# Don't
## *date him...*

A Guide to Not Dating the Wrong Man

DR. TYRA HODGE, PH.D.

ISBN: 979-8-412-32667-2 (Paperback)
ISBN: 978-0-578-36854-2 (Hardcover)
ISBN: 978-0-578-36856-6 (eBook)

# Contents

# INTRODUCTION

## Why should anyone listen to me?

There are a lot of dating guides out there, so why should you be interested in reading this one? I am not a relationship counselor, nor is my Ph. D. in psychology. However, it is in education. So, what sets me apart from everyone else? Well, I am an expert on bad dates.

Over the years, I have been a waitress, a dancer, a single woman, and a single mother. I was an abused wife whose husband occasionally disappeared for days at a time. I was a teacher, a School District Behavior Specialist, assistant principal, radio show host, and now the Founder and President of a non-profit organization that reaches out to parents. Eventually, I learned to make better choices, but during this time,

I became a guru of dating – with both good and bad results. I went on some great dates, and I ventured on many of the world's worst dates. After telling one of my girlfriends about one of these "worst dates," and reducing her to tears of laughter (see "Don't Date Him if His Farts are Toxic to Your Health"), I decided to write down some of my stories. From there, I was able to generate a list of "don't date him if…" and when the list quickly became 78 items long, it became clear that I needed to share my knowledge with women of the world.

As I have gotten older, I have seen many women I love go through divorces that may have been prevented if they had put a little more thought into their long-term relationships while they were still dating. Although there is no way to predict the obstacles that might come up over the course of the marriage, choosing a good man as their partner is a woman's best chance at a happy marriage. Similarly, some people are good at hiding things, and a person might only reveal their true colors after marriage. Or, as people change, minor issues might turn into major habits and addictions.

However, most of the time, there are signs long before the exchange of rings that this relationship is headed downhill. The key to success is to see these signs and stop dating that person immediately because once a woman is "in love," there is no talking sense into her.

Rather than noticing the signs, the women choose to make excuses, ignore the signs, and consequently put up with years of crap.

**Don't Date Him** is not meant to bash all men or to make women feel so disillusioned that they never want to go on another date again. Rather, this book is meant to set simple guidelines to help you spot a bad mate before he gets so involved in your life that you can't figure out how to make him leave, or worse, you don't want him to leave. I speak from my personal experience and from the experience of others. I am offering this experience and my very own, very funny, "bad date" stories in hopes that you will not make the same mistakes I made. After all, we all have choices when it comes to the men we fall in love with – we can choose not to date them.

*- Dr. Tyra Hodge.*

## Don't Date Him If One of His Parents Tells You Not Too (Losers)

There are men who think they are entitled to waste your time. If you pay enough attention, you can easily spot them and shove them out the door. Our emotions have a reputation of clouding our judgment, and in the heat of the moment, we may overlook certain things which…well, we probably shouldn't and end up putting up with a guy we should have left cold-turkey much sooner.

So, before you get emotionally involved with the guy, pay attention to how he is at work. How does he own up to his mistakes? Pay heed to the two cents his parents may have given you about him and whether he follows up on rules and regulations.

Now that we have set the starting base for the book,

I will be providing you with plenty of situations that you as a Dating Woman will likely find yourself in and what to do once you're in them.

## Don't date him if he quits at everything.

I dated two different men who dropped out of school in the ninth grade. They both stated how hard it was and said they didn't have time for it anymore. They wanted to go to work and start making money. Well, funnily enough, neither of these men could keep a job, wife, car, apartment, or even a fish. Their lives would make a great country song. They never had money, and they never showed any sign of responsibility. Let's call the first guy Jeremy because that's his real name. I had a pregnancy scare with Jeremy. As soon as this guy found out there was a chance I was pregnant, he disappeared. He literally left everything in his apartment and skipped town. He called me a week later and told me how sorry he was, and I concurred. He continued to call until I convinced him that I truly meant it when I said: "Go to hell." Several weeks later, I discovered Jeremy had a baby on the way with another girl. When she told him that she was pregnant, guess what happened? That's right, y'all. He disappeared on her, too. He left that poor girl high, dry, alone, and pregnant.

The second person I dated, a high school dropout, could never keep a job past three months. He never tried to get a GED and liked people to take care of him. He also liked to complain about what his friends and family had compared to himself and at no time did he try to earn anything of his own or try to better himself. This is problematic in relationships because such a mentality is not motivational for you or your children. Parents want their children to believe that they can go after anything and achieve anything because they worked for it. This is not the message that drop-outs send. My disclaimer: a person that gets their GED IS a graduate.

Both men were quitters. A job could never satisfy them because they weren't content with themselves. I also noticed that both men thought living in an unsafe home was acceptable. Some people don't have a choice, but a healthy man has the same opportunity as others. They both became huge drug users. It is important to remember that a student who starts quitting at a young age can have a hard time placing a value on commitment, and they may relinquish responsibility during crucial times.

## Don't date him if he can't keep a job.

I have now learned my lesson about what a man means when he says he is "between jobs." Translation: his sorry ass probably hasn't had a job for a long time. A man who can't keep a job can't keep a woman. If he can't keep a woman, he can't keep a family. I married a man who had a difficult time keeping a job. After I got married and had my first child with my first husband, he was adamant about staying home with the baby while working. Staying home with the baby sounded great!

However, as the pregnancy progressed, he was home as much as I was. He was either too sleepy to work, or he just lost his job. At the end of my pregnancy, I received a wonderful job offer at the local school district. After all, one of us had to work. I practically worked until my water broke and was back to work two weeks later. I would wake up every two hours for the baby's feedings during the night while my husband slept. I would work all day. Lather, rinse and repeat every day. My marriage didn't last, but the position I took as a teacher's assistant had blossomed and helped pay the bills until I finished college. I had become a teacher, a Behavior Specialist, a writer, a doctoral student, and a speaker. The man I married (and divorced) does not have a job to this day. He still lives with his mom. How does the saying go? What doesn't kill you makes you a little less stupid next time.

It is indeed very important to know the necessary traits to look for in selecting a man to date. For example, if a man cannot keep a job for three months continuously, he is likely not consistent in other decisions. A man who understands the importance of a job will not leave a job without a good reason (and without another job waiting). Consistency is a very important factor that a woman should consider when looking for a man to date. A man who is not consistent will easily shy away from responsibilities. If he does not appreciate the idea of a hard day's work, it can be an indicator that he doesn't have the capacity to make mature decisions. For instance, today, he can say I love you and tomorrow decide he isn't sure anymore. A relationship is hard work. He needs to appreciate the importance of hard work in all aspects of his life. Instead, a man who CAN keep a job for more than three months CAN keep a woman for that long. He CAN make decisions and be consistent. This type of man would be the ideal candidate for a woman who is looking to date. He always takes care of his family, and he does not engage himself in love affairs outside his marriage. A stable man can ensure a happy family, which is emulated by many. Besides, what girl wants a man that lives off her money and won't contribute?

## Don't date him if he blames his faults on others.

Taking responsibility for our actions is one way that people can find positive growth within themselves. When a person can truly understand and care about how their actions can affect someone else, they are making progress towards becoming a date-worthy man.

I had a female friend whose boyfriend was always getting into trouble. He never took credit for being a first-class idiot. He constantly had poor excuses for his mistakes, including when he was caught cheating, and she would make excuses for him.

Finally, I instructed my friend to tell him to go; it was okay to blame her for staying out too late because she gave him the debit card. Sure enough, the next time he stayed out late, he agreed that he would not have stayed out late if he did not have access to the money. My friend finally saw the light and laughed in his face. In fact, she laughed all the way to my apartment with her bag of clothes as she left him for good.

It is very important for everyone to take responsibility for their own actions. In many instances, some people find it difficult to take responsibility because it may be hard to face that you just may suck as a person. This discredits them in the eyes of many. Only through taking responsibility for our actions can people see change within us. I think most women like men who are responsible and always ready to take responsibility for their actions, both good and bad. A man who does not take responsibility can't make a good family man. He will always shift the blame to a woman, even when he is clearly at fault. A man who cares about his family is aware of what he does since his actions may affect his partner and children. Therefore, it is of great importance for everyone to be careful about how he behaves. In most ended marriages, women take responsibility more than men. Most men prefer to shift the blame to their wives rather than take fault and grow as a person.

## Don't date him if he tells little lies.

A liar is a liar, is a liar. There was this guy I was quite fond of in Bible school. He was handsome but was the epitome of Attention Deficit Hyperactivity Disorder (ADHD). OK. I do tend to tell wild stories; my stories are true! This particular guy, however, would lie about small things. For instance, I had a car, and he claimed it was his dream car. He just "had to" drive it. In the nine months that I dated him, I noticed that he said that to two other people in my presence. Mind you, my car was a Hyundai Excel and was what many people consider was a throwaway car. The other girls he told the same story to (emphasis on the girls) similarly had cars that most people would not consider to be dream cars. Sounds like a petty detail, right? Well, I eventually found a letter from one of these women, stating that she could not return his love and their relationship had to stop because she was engaged to someone else. Maybe, if I had paid attention to these "small" fibs, I could have recognized the potential for larger lies as well.

All women hate lies and false hopes. In most cases, men will lie to win the confidence of a lady by telling her what they want to hear. She is then given a false sense of hope, with dreams of a future romance that will end in an everlasting commitment.

Lying to a person to date them ultimately leads to a broken heart and takes away a personal choice because they chose a person under pretenses.

> Don't date him if he continually tells you stories about himself that you don't enjoy.

After the "party" phase of my life had come to an end, I began going to church. At church, I met an ex-professional baseball player who asked me out on a date.

Mind you, I had recently decided to quit the "party girl" life and was attempting to stay on the right path. This retired baseball player thought his past partying and cocaine use was so admirable and "cool." During the entire duration of one of our dates, he talked about drugs which were a challenging ordeal for someone who was trying to reform.

Another warning sign: if he continually tells you he is a lady's man, turn around, walk out the door, and run. He will never be satisfied with just one woman and will constantly need to prove that he still has "it" at the cost of your feelings. For example, my friend, Laura, told me her boyfriend frequently brought up the beautiful girls he used to date. She began to feel insecure about her appearance, and it took time for her to realize that his words were, in fact, a reflection of his insecurities. Although it is human nature to have insecurities, it is crucial never to become involved with someone who points out those insecurities. A relationship is about breaking down those walls of insecurity, not bringing those insecurities out.

Certain men make a habit of praising themselves. This is a concern that deserves attention. As women, it is natural to crave an occasional compliment. In a competition to win a woman's confidence, a man should remember to make her feel special and not only focus on himself. Several men like talking about other women they have dated in the past, which can frequently be a turn-off to women. Others go to extremes in    explaining how they used to make love in their past love affairs and the wonderful experiences they went through. Remember, every woman has the right to be unique; in other words, do not tolerate listening to a significant other talk about past love affairs. If a man is serious about you, he will be conscious of what he says and how he treats you. Your story is just as important as his. Make sure he appreciates it!

Many women want to hear as many stories about their significant other as possible. Listening to the cute guy across the table talk about his 7th birthday party? Sure. Listening to the cute guy across the table give detailed accounts of exploits with ex-lovers? We'll pass on that.

## Don't date him if one of his parents tells you not to.

You will always have those mothers who think no one is right for their son. You know the ones I'm talking about: the lazy, pathetic man who, despite constant failures, whose mother continues to make excuses about the evil world attacking her poor, innocent son. There is nothing anyone could ever do to please these women. They will never accept you because she views you as a threat, coming to take her baby away. Believe it or not, I never had much of this problem. As a matter of fact, I had a couple of mothers visit me at the club I worked at, and tip! Although you should always walk away from a man with "mommy-issues," from my experience, if his parents tell you that YOU are too good for HIM, don't even question it. RUN.

For example, after I had given up dancing and started college, I met a guy's family that liked me. His dad was unnaturally curious as to what I was doing with his son. He told me to run and never look back. He told me that his son was a piece of crap. He was adamant about the fact that his son would ruin my life. Guess what? His son was a piece of crap.

Although all parents are different, some parents can be very truthful. Usually, fathers tend to be slightly more aware of both the positive and negative regarding their kids, and it is important to heed their words. On the other hand, mothers are always protective of their sons and daughters, and it may be more difficult to hear the truth from them. Regardless, LISTEN to what the parents say; it can save you loads of heartache.

Listening to his parents can singlehandedly help you steer clear away from wasting further time with the guy you are currently dating. Take the following scenario: You meet a guy, and you hit it off. You're seeing sunshine and daisies everywhere and sending text messages back and forth filled with lovey-dovey emojis. You're starting to wonder if this could have a future with this man, and then the big day comes. You meet his family. And they tell you NOT to date their son.

Now pay attention, because his parent will not take you to a secluded corner of the room and give you details about their son being notorious for leading women on. Instead, the warnings will be subtle and hint at his jerkiness.

For example:

"Oh, nice to meet you dear; Jim often brings his friends over for tea. It is a shame he never sticks with one girl."

*What?*

Let's take a moment to analyze these words of wisdom further:

Our parents are our Raison D'être. If it were not for them, we would not even exist. As people who have birthed us and watched us grow, they know us better than anyone. They have a very good idea of our temperament, how we are likely to respond in one situation, how likely we are to follow up with our plans and promises, etc. They have been with us through it all.

Our parents have a very good idea of what kind of a person we essentially are, and when Jim's parents drop a crucial hint about Jim's behavior, you should not let it go without pondering over it.

I am not advocating that you dump Jim's sorry behind there and then. You were just given a clue, a kind of puzzle piece, and your job is to be on guard and follow that lead. Do not get emotionally invested in the guy before you know how these pieces fit together and that Jim is someone worth your time and energy.

And if you find him not worth it, you know what to do. Move on.

## Don't date him if he breaks the law.

All your life, you have done the right thing. Following the rules brought you this far. Why would you change that?

You may have read the story of America's most famous criminal couple, Bonnie Parker and Clyde Barrow. Perhaps, you haven't. They were two young Texans whose involvement in crime imprinted them on the consciousness of Americans in the early 1930s.

Their names became associated with an era with an image of women brandishing automatic rifles alongside men robbing banks and driving off with squeaky cars. They lived their lives on the fast lane because it would be so short.

The truth is that this image was far from reality like we find with many couples who are involved in crime. Although they were one of the first outlaw media stars, their fame soon turned sour, and their lives ended in a bloody police shootout.

It is common sense for a person to avoid dating a guy with a penchant for crime or getting into serious trouble with the law. The risks are too high.

When it comes to love and other human emotions, common sense may not always be enough to dissuade someone from still having feelings for a person engaged in criminal activity, but you will soon realize that such relationships are more likely to have more struggles, risks, and repercussions compared to the stable relationship.

The person you want to be involved with may have once been on the straight and narrow, but through some events, they landed in situations involving criminal activity and even spent time behind bars. Whether such a relationship will be for a short instance or become a long-term commitment, there are many ways it will affect your life and relationships with people around you.

If you choose to be involved with a guy who has been incarcerated for very serious crimes, your judgment and sanity may regularly be questioned, and this could bring a lot of negativity into your life. Such a situation can affect your social life and relationships outside of your primary romantic one, employment, and other areas.

For people with children, even their own kids may feel the brunt of their actions if other parents find out and don't want their children talking to or playing with someone whose parent is associated with a known criminal.

In the worst-case scenario, you may initially decide to be with someone with a criminal background but eventually, change your mind.

When you consider substance abuse, violence, and the baggage commonly associated with people with criminal records, choosing to leave someone involved in criminal behavior may put your wellbeing in danger. You may place yourself at the risk of being stalked, hurt in retaliation, or even have your loved ones put at risk out of anger because you chose to walk away.

This factor should strongly be considered when choosing to love and remain with someone with a potentially hazardous personality and criminal lifestyle.

Being involved with such a person may be exciting at first, but eventually, when the excitement dies down, you may have doubts or concerns or maybe just need some support when struggling through the difficult parts of your relationship with them.

If some personal experience would help you see

the need to avoid dating someone who breaks the law, here is one:

I knew a girl; let's call her Sally. Sally had a boyfriend; she knew he was selling prescription drugs on the side to supplement his minimum wage job, but it didn't bother her enough to stop her from dating him. We all hoped Sally would "date up," but we never realized how his actions could cause negative consequences for her. She allowed him to use her car from time to time, and one day she was speeding to work and got pulled over. The officer decided to check her car. The police officer found a bag of pills and a handgun under her seat. Sally went to jail. Now, her charges would have been dropped against her if her boyfriend had come forward to claim his items, but of course, he didn't. Sally was hit with a drug charge. It has been years since I have seen her. The moral of the story is that, like herpes, drug charges don't ever go away.

Women should be very careful when in the dating world. They need to make the right decisions about a man whom they see as a potential future husband. Nowadays, it is easily possible to become involved in criminal activities, such as drug trafficking and other crimes. Any interaction with drugs could become a serious problem and should be avoided. A person involved in the drug scene could easily end up in jail and be thrown behind bars for years at a time, and this prevents any possibility of familial stability.

Furthermore, if a man is jailed for any reason, he leaves the entire burden to a woman. This leads to a bad childhood upbringing and ruins the family structure. Equally, if the man is violent in any way, the woman should consider leaving him if he does not change IMMEDIATELY. Remember, your kids will look to their parents to see what is acceptable, and if they see dangerous activities as acceptable, they may begin following in those footsteps.

## Don't date him if you think that he will change.

It's quite amusing that men often consider marrying a woman, hoping she never changes, while a woman considers marrying a man she hopes she can change. Unfortunately, the reality is that you can do everything for people – support, inspire and even educate them, but you can't change them.

Just like me, you've probably had that one person in your life that you always found yourself say, "If only they would…" Day after day, month after month, year after year – you loved, worried, and cared about them.

Maybe this is an ex-boyfriend. Maybe you saw them messing up big time. Drinking too much, cheating on you, and regularly blowing all their money on an addiction. Maybe you kept buying them books that they never read, or you dragged them to a therapist that they refused to go to. You probably pulled them aside and gave them the hands-on-the-shoulder pep talk you are supposed to do. Maybe you offered them a loan or two. These efforts never worked, but you kept thinking:

"Am I not enough? If only they would get their life together…"

We all have that person in our lives. Caring for them

and loving them hurts deeply. Losing them also hurts. We, therefore, decide that the only way to salvage this emotional trainwreck is to somehow change them.

My answer whenever I am asked, "How do I get him/her to change?" is this, "You can't."

What was that saying about teaching an old dog new tricks? Oh yeah, you can't. You can't make him change. You can inspire him to change, support, and educate him towards change, but you can't make him change.

There are many reasons why you shouldn't date him because you think he will change. Basically, to make him do something he is unwilling to do, even if it's for his own good, requires either coercion or manipulation. Doing this would require you to intervene in his life in a way that violates his boundary, which will eventually damage the relationship more than it helps. Hence, it's best to stay away.

I learned the hard way not to put faith in anyone except God. Once upon a time, I was engaged, and I had such high hopes for him. He promised to change "if only" I would stay with him and help him change. In the short time I was with him, his family had said there were changes taking place in him. I believed that I was his savior. We went to church together, and his family loved and praised me for that. Although we were going to church, he was still a demon. I put a lot of time into helping him; however, he didn't give a darn about anyone other than himself. We were both caught up in a twisted, sick game of fantasy. I wanted so much to have someone love me enough that they would be willing to change. He wanted to see someone love him so much; she would be willing to keep him, no matter what. Through this experience, I learned that people must want to change for themselves rather than for another person. You can't change a man, and if you are waiting for him to change, you are wasting your life.

In most relationships, you will find that many boundary violations often go unnoticed because we do them with good intentions. For example, Mike lost his job and decided to spend the rest of the year indoors watching TV and feeling sorry for himself. Abigail started filling out job applications for Mike. Soon, she began to yell at him, calling him names and guilt-tripping him for not making any move to get a job. She did these things believing they would give Mike an extra oomph of motivation.

While her intentions seem good and noble, this type of behavior often has consequences and will ultimately backfire.

In every sense, it's a boundary violation. Although it comes from the place of concern and love, it's taking responsibility for another person's actions and emotions and damages relationships.

A wise lady should be careful with the kind of

men she decides to trust. Be cautious with whom you decide to invest your time, and if you see traits you are uncomfortable with, LEAVE. Rather, you should be ready to take measures immediately. For example, many men will promise a woman that they will stop drinking beer if they are engaged to get married; however, if you don't like his habits now, don't date him hoping for that change! It is nearly impossible for an adult to adopt a new lifestyle, especially if he is not willing and dedicated to change.

Try to imagine how difficult it is to change even one thing about yourself. Now, imagine someone else asking you to change when you don't want to change. Do you honestly believe that your love alone is enough to get someone to change his personality completely? No! It does not work that way. Men are practical people, but they are also selfish. It is possible for men who were completely astray to come back to the right path, but this desire to change must come from within.

They might quit smoking. The man might stop doing drugs. They might start giving you the time you deserve, but the first step of making a change is realizing there is a problem. They must realize why they need to change and how their behavior is negatively impacting the relationship. In other words, should you date a man with hopes of him changing his ways and becoming a better man? *NO!*

## Don't Date Him If He Breaks Things When He's Mad. (Angry Men)

Over the years of my career, I have seen and heard women have become more vocal about mental health than their male counterparts. Naturally, this has raised some questions in my mind that I am sure you have also pondered over.

1. *Why do men find it hard to openly express their emotions and concerns about mental health-related matters?*
2. *What keeps men from being vocal about issues that hugely affect them?*
3. *Is there some relationship between emotional intelligence and gender?*

Although emotional intelligence (EQ) is a concept

that has been with us from time immemorial, it matters in relationships because it can be used to strengthen the bond with your man, increase intimacy and build a love that lasts, it is alien to most men. There is a general misconception that men who talk about their feelings and are emotionally expressive are too "feminine."

I once dated a man who showed me some of the poems he had written. When I asked him why he stopped composing poetry, he told me he did not want others to think he was an incompetent man who resorted to poetry. If you ask me, that is some deranged logic.

I have discovered that most women I have counseled have faced challenges in their relationships due to a dearth of emotionally intelligent men. Thanks to societal definitions of masculinity, it is difficult to come across men who regard emotional health with the concern it truly deserves.

It's therefore telling that the majority of the challenges around masculinity are linked to predetermined cultural norms, and they tend to be identical in many parts of the world. Most of the men that you will come across will have absolutely zero ideas on how to deal with their emotional side, let alone tackle your emotional wellbeing.

Although central to our daily experiences as humans, our emotions are simply impulses that pull us toward or away from a range of actions. This is why anger, although a negative emotion essential to our wellbeing, does not always have to be expressed in a harmful way.

It is perfect and acceptable to feel angry. It often helps us identify our boundaries, what will and won't be acceptable in our relationships and situations with people. We generally feel angry when someone crosses this line. How we respond, behave and handle the emotion when we feel it matters a lot.

Most men don't consider the importance of handling emotions safely; therefore, they do not know how to express it the right way. The most they can do is identify an emotion for what it is, but they are not equipped with the right skills to handle it. Consequently, when you date an emotionally immature man, you see such severe mood swings that you often wonder what the true side is.

The most you will get out of a man like that would be, "It's nothing, I'm just really moody."

So, what defines emotionally intelligent men?

Men who show emotional intelligence can recognize, understand and respond appropriately to emotions in themselves and others. The ability to be self-aware and empathize is uncommon and requires that one must first recognize and adequately manage their emotions.

We live in a world suffering from a breakdown of

emotional intelligence, a world where emotional abuse is a very real problem. It is often used by abusers to control another person by using emotions to manipulate, shame, embarrass and blame them. Emotionally abusive relationships are generally characterized by patterns of abusive words and bullying behaviors that tear down your self-esteem and undermine your mental health.

While mental or emotional abuse can occur in any relationship, it is common in dating and married relationships. It's one of the hardest forms of abuse to recognize because there may not be physical bruises that would act as evidence. But never downplay the seriousness of emotional abuse either. It chips away at the victim's self-worth, and they begin to second guess their perceptions and reality and feel trapped.

"Sticks and stones may break your bones, but words can never hurt." False, words can truly hurt.

Every time we read about another senseless killing or domestic violence, it's a sign that emotional intelligence has gone awry. The worst part about emotional abuse is that the only method of treatment is time. The healing time to recover after hurtful words said in a weak moment can take months or years to overcome. Avoid this situation and make sure always to evaluate a man on his ability to not only handle his emotions but to handle yours as well.

## Don't date him if he switches emotions like Dr. Jekyll and Mr. Hyde.

I once met a family where the husband projected a very wholesome outer image. This man was the picture of humility and modesty. With time, his behaviors soon showed an entirely different side. He turned out to be wife beater; he was both verbally and physically abusive to his family whenever he got angry.

Men are human, so they will try to put their best foot forward at the beginning. So, it's often tough to initially see who they really are. Sometimes, it's not an issue of a two-faced personality, as much as it is that you're not suited for one another and shouldn't be romantically involved.

Victims of the Dr. Jekyll and Mr. Hyde relationship often have difficulties figuring out which one is real and which one is the anomaly. Women tend to deny the distasteful traits in a man because it's easier for us to believe that the person we like is truly their "better self."

While you shouldn't overlook the good favor of judging the faults and inadequacies in a person or relationship, when you see something that doesn't sit well with you, you must ensure that you give it the attention it deserves and make a decision on it.

Everyone has a bad day now and then. One single meltdown is not what I am talking about. I am talking about someone who has dramatic changes in mood without any reason. This type of person may have a mental disorder, whether or not they are aware of it. Mental disorders left unattended can be dangerous to the person and hazardous to you. These people are not necessarily "bad" people, but they do need to seek professional help. Many people from time to time may need to seek outside help. When in doubt, seek medical assistance.

It is very important for any man to be able to control his emotions. A man who keeps on switching his emotions does not add any value to the family. Rather, he leads the family to more problems. Men who are mostly driven by emotions may cause problems because they do not know how to solve problems through dialogue. Instead, they act out of emotions. A good family man should be careful when dealing with his children and wife at home. He should always make sure that he does not cause trouble at home due to stress in the workplace. Women should be careful to detect men who switch their emotions very fast and act when they do.

## Don't date him if he has a serious case of road rage.

When we date and overlook red flags like this, we are setting ourselves up for heartache. If this person is habitually engaged in rage with people he will never meet and, in the larger picture, did little or nothing, how will he respond to you if you did something of significance to upset him?

Children pick up on a lot of things we say as adults. For example, I was with a friend and her five-year-old son going to the store. After she drove for a while, her son said, "Mom, where are all the scumbags?" My friend immediately stopped the car, turned around, and exclaimed, "What?! Where did you learn that word from?" Her son said, "When Dad drives, there are scumbags everywhere. They are all gone when you drive. Where did they go?"

Another story came from a manager at Home Depot that I went out with a couple of times. He was a very handsome gentleman who was confined to a wheelchair. While out one night, he told me the story of how he came to be in a wheelchair. He once dated a stripper with a bad temper. She succumbed to this temper in an episode of road rage near the Galveston sea wall. This uncontrolled rage incident left her dead, and him bound to a wheelchair for the rest of his life. The roles can reverse at any time. So, watch out!

## Don't date him if he can't express his feelings.

One other important thing I have learned is that if he can't express how he feels about you, then he probably does not feel much about you at all. Why waste your time with someone who does not return your feelings? Trust me; you don't want him to lie and say he feels something when he doesn't! I have seen it often with middle school students I've worked with for years. A young boy will tell a girl all these sweet nothings, the young girl gives him her virginity and then he is off to her friend.

Sometimes, this behavior from middle school will continue right into their adult lives. My friend, Christina, was with a guy for eight months. This guy had a great sense of humor and was very charming, but when it came to expressing emotions, he should have worn a giant dunce hat. He would tell Christina that spending time with her was enough to show how he felt and question why she needed to hear how he felt?

Christina is not alone; there are many women who stay in relationships where their emotional needs are not met. When their partners question them as to why it is necessary for them to seek emotional validation from them, they are putting the women down for being "emotionally needy." Different people require different things from relationships. For most women, emotional support or even validation is vital. Actions might speak louder than words, but that doesn't mean words aren't important! Eventually, there comes a time when those emotional needs won't be met, and leaving is the only available option.

## Don't date him if he gives you the silent treatment.

I have never really understood how staying silent can help resolve anything. True, in the heat of the moment, silence helps, but what about after the heat of the moment, when your guy still refuses to break the silence? Relationships thrive on communication, and if you are with someone who considers silent treatment as a healthy coping mechanism, you need to leave him and his silence alone for good.

You have a fight with your man, and you wait for things to calm down. Things have calmed down, except they have REALLY calmed down. We're talking; the guy goes on an unannounced boycott. You reach out to him, only to receive no reply. He bluntly refuses to communicate with you or acknowledge your presence.

The truth is that the silent treatment can be a form of emotional abuse and an unproductive way of communicating or dealing with disagreements within a relationship. People who use it do it to control, manipulate, and even punish their partners. What then is the rationale for the silent treatment if a man claims he loves you?

## Don't date him if he likes to break things when he's mad.

If a man breaks things when he gets mad, it is usually due to a loss of power. To gain control, he may break things to scare you, or it may be an attempt to control you. Physical violence is a dangerous game that no one wins. If a person breaks items, he may break things that you hold valuable too. I once dated a guy who would break things that my mother and sister had given to me. Even scarier than this is the consideration that when breaking items no longer seems to give him the power he wants, he may begin breaking limbs on your body.

Do not date a man if he likes to break things when he's mad. Breaking things has many disadvantages, and a man who cares about his family will not behave in such a manner. A man who tends to break things may damage assets in the house, leading to huge losses. There are many ways of resolving conflicts or relieving stress; however; breaking things does not solve any problem.

## Don't date him if he hurts animals.

I shouldn't even have to explain why anyone who hurts animals is a no-good douche bag, but I will anyway. Hurting animals is bad juju. Psychology has a lot to say about this topic.

Acts of cruelty towards animals go beyond indications of a minor personality flaw. It is symptomatic of deep mental trouble. Studies show that people who commit acts of cruelty to animals don't just stop them; most of them also hurt their fellow humans.

Some folks use the hurting of animals as another way to control a person. If an abusive person understands they can't hurt you, they may go after a pet. This is a dangerous person! If this person is young and is hurting animals for enjoyment, don't even go near him! Forget that. Just call the police. This person may very well get bored with animals and soon bury people in his back yard. History is replete with serial killers who first directed their violent tendencies at animals, and there is sufficient evidence that murderers and rapists often start out by hurting or killing animals as kids.

Albert DeSalvo (the "Boston Strangler") killed more than 10 women, trapped animals, and shot arrows at them through boxes in his youth. Nikolas Cruz and Luke Woodham, High-School killers, tortured animals before they began their shooting sprees.

Shrugging off such cruelty to animals in your partner is like ignoring a ticking time bomb. Abuse of any living being is unacceptable and endangers everyone. Therefore, don't even consider dating a man with such an attitude.

## Don't date him if he likes to start fights — or finishes them.

Arguments happen. No two people are the same, and it is just not possible to see eye to eye on everything with someone.

However, when the fights (whether they involve you or do not involve you) start to happen too often, you need to take a step back and see what is happening.

Obviously, the guy is having difficulty controlling his temper. And very soon, it is going to come out on you, too.

You may think you can handle them; however, you

will find that even a little misunderstanding will escalate, and you will start resenting him and yourself.

I went out with this guy on three separate dates. He was in a type of conflict on each date. The first, someone was looking at him funny. The second date included a fight with his uncle. The third time resulted in him getting kicked out of my favorite bar. He wanted me to leave with him, but hey, I wasn't going to get banned from my favorite bar for anyone. Sometimes, you must make a choice. Besides, who wants to go to jail or to be seen with the person always getting into fights?

## Don't date him if he seems to lose his temper.

It's typical for little kids to throw temper tantrums and express their feelings in a loud, out-of-control way because they don't know any better. But, as we grow older, we start to learn that keeping our anger in check is a life skill essential to maintaining good relationships. Unfortunately, plenty of adults never learn this skill, and it's in your best interest to avoid them at all costs.

Getting into a fight with your guy at some point in your relationship is inevitable. How this is dealt with, and the way your boyfriend addresses problems shows his feelings towards you. If the first thing he chooses to do is to corner you and start attacking you with hurtful words, he doesn't respect you.

A person who can't control his temper is a time bomb waiting to explode. With a person like this, you always have to walk on eggshells when he is around. You may find yourself going overboard to pacify this person, but there is never any use. He will use any excuse to throw a huge hissy fit when he doesn't get his way, making a perfect reenactment of a big baby.

Don't date a man if he seems to lose his temper. It is advisable for a man always to control his temper. Men who lose their temper are capable of doing unthinkable things that might negatively impact their life or the life of family members. Real men control their tempers. Unless they need to kick the ass of someone messing with their family. Self-control is of great significance for a woman who intends to have a well-functioning family. A man who loses his temper brings shame to the family, which may contribute to a bad reputation. A well-behaved man is respected by everyone, and he understands the importance of earning this respect. It is very risky for a woman to date a hot-tempered man because he can easily fight with the woman for no real reason, causing serious consequences. Women should keep away from such men.

## Don't date him if he is jealous for no reason

Envy is one of the seven deadly sins. Jealousy can do

horrible things to a man or woman. I once knew a woman named Susan, who was abused by her boyfriend for saying "hi" to another man. When Susan's boyfriend would have friends over, he would lock her in their bedroom. Demented, I know, but true.

Envy is dangerous, no matter the circumstance. For example, a woman may be more intelligent than a man, which may cause the man to be extra sensitive about this issue. This fact may create feelings of bitterness, which may ultimately make him do something to affect the family adversely. For example, he might decide not to help the woman financially, claiming that she can also handle her finances since she is very bright. Later, this might lead to a family break-up.

Possessiveness is NOT cute. I know so many women who marvel over how "possessive" guys seem to be over them...well, when this escalates into a full-on lockdown, trust me, it would not be so cute after all. Some people also tend to confuse possessiveness with a concern which is such a common error!

For example, your boyfriend may not worry about who you hang out with because they trust you, whereas you can take this "lack of investment" as a lack of concern. His lack of investigation always means that he does not care. If you happen to come across a man who trusts you to do your own thing without questioning you nonstop, then remember this: you have landed a gem of a person. Hold on to him!

## Don't date him if he throws temper tantrums.

Dating someone who likes to throw temper tantrums because he doesn't get his way is not a good situation. Someone who is quick to anger and throws tantrums sees fights as a means to an end. Who can deliver the most scathing remarks and leave the other speechless in the end? Who can win this tussle of words? This may sound twisted, but it's the way angry people process things.

Talk about embarrassing! When I was right out of high school, I dated a guy who liked to hit things when he got mad. He had a typical temper tantrum: scream, cuss, and hit things. We worked at a Christian camp, and when he found out that he would not be allowed to come back the following year, he went through the biggest fit you had ever seen in public, outside, at a church camp. The other people would look at him and then look at me. Look at him again, then look at me. Politicians get it right when they date; they date someone with a clean history and someone who knows how to keep face when something bad happens.

You need a person who can keep their cool. You don't want their actions to reflect on you.

## Don't date him if he is way older than you.

Yes, age is just a number, but let me justify why this number is important.

Being with someone twice your age can result in a few challenges. Not only would you have to put up with his poor hearing and find yourself repeating things repeatedly, but there might also be compatibility issues. He is old, you are young, and it is only natural that you want different things from life.

Your interests, hobbies, and overall mindset are different. You will also have different goals because you are at different stages of your lives.

Furthermore, for him, everything is a bit "been there and done that" kind of situation. You want to go to a rave party which begins when his bedtime starts! A good portion of his personal history is tied to past events, so it wouldn't be strange that you don't know the same songs or like the same movies. These can take a toll on the relationship over time because being in a relationship requires having some things in common.

While couples with age differences can take

advantage of the situation by embracing gaps in knowledge and using it to learn new things, cultural references can also serve as a reminder of the difference between ages.

Having said that, some women prefer to date men who are significantly older. Their argument is, of course, "men are like wine; they get better with age." I guess, at the end of it, it all boils down to preferences, but in my opinion, if you are a 25-year-old woman who is interested in a 60- year old man, just know what you are getting yourself into. However, I do prefer men a little older. I like the distinguished look.

DON'T
DATE HIM

3

## Don't Date Him If He Gets Wasted More than Twice a Year. (Drugs & Alcohol)

The guy you should be with should understand the concept of drinking responsibly. Sure, getting wasted in Vegas once in a year (or twice) may be the thing of fun for some people, but if this is more of a habit than once in a blue moon, that guy might not be the best for dating.

Let's break this down.

I love a glass of wine with friends and family; it makes the dinner jokes so much more hilarious. However, anyone who is old enough to drink should know how to drink appropriately! Most likely, everyone who has tried a drink has overindulged once or twice over the course of a lifetime. But, if you or someone you are dating is falling drunk every time you drink, you need to stop and get help. You want a dignified man, not a boyfriend who will fall into the Thanksgiving turkey.

Drunk as a skunk has never been my motto. Someone who has a drinking problem can flip out on you any second. We have all heard of men beating women up because they were too drunk and let their temper get the better of them. Alcoholics are not fun to be around. If anything, they are a liability to everyone around them. YOU would constantly be babysitting him every time the two of you were out. YOU would be the one ensuring he is not throwing up everywhere. YOU would be the one praying for your life every time he got behind the wheel.

There are some people who do not know how to have fun in places where alcohol is not involved. Drunkards are a major buzzkill and a huge red flag. As much as you would not mind downing a drink or two, you should be with someone who is equally fun to be around when he has no whiskey in his veins. So, just a piece of advice, when you are dating someone, make sure to try out activities like hiking or paragliding to see his alcohol-free, adventurous side.

## Don't date him if he abuses chemical substances.

Drug addiction often becomes a compulsive habit and a need despite users knowing it is harmful. What follows addiction is its impact on the individual and the people around them. It interferes with every area of the user's life, leading to heartache, a damaged body, lying, guilt, missed opportunities, and most painful of all – broken relationships.

For one, the person you're dating needs to have respect for the law. If you have children, they are watching you, and they will not do what you say, but what you do. The sins of the children are always worse than their ancestors. Drugs do kill brain cells, and when a person is addicted to drugs, their only concern is drugs. Drugs will deaden the consciousness of a person. To this person, the only mission in life is the next high. They may keep you around just so they can have food, shelter, and money.

Don't you want and deserve more?

Honesty and good communication are essentials associated with healthy relationships – but you will not find either of these when addiction is in the picture. Instead, you will find the following in the conversation:

- Denial or lies of drug or alcohol abuse

- Manipulation
- Defensiveness when drug use comes up
- A "flight or fight" reaction if addiction or therapy is discussed

One of my less dazzling moments happened while I was dating a guy with an extreme devotion to cocaine. We dated for three months, and I had three different DVD players disappear. By the third time, I finally realized he was stealing and selling them to get money for cocaine. I quickly made *him* dissolve.

You don't want to be in a situation with a guy where it feels like drugs are winning and your relationship is losing.

> Don't date him if he makes plans of sobering up but never follows through.

If he wanted to quit, he would quit right now. Men who make up random, open-ended timelines for quitting will not abandon their drug addiction! Do not get talked into believing their false promises. Women have lost years that could have been good times. Instead, many years are squandered on a person who has laid down his life on drugs.

Addicts and their actions are completely beyond your control – it will always be this way. Therefore, it's important that you know the difference between what you can change and what you can't change. Knowing this will strengthen you.

If you choose to buy into their belief that they can't exist without you and their addiction, you will be setting yourself up for manipulation. The more you allow yourself to be manipulated, the more they will manipulate you.

I have seen women put up with men who are alcoholics and substance abusers for long periods, hoping and praying that on some fateful day, their man will have a change of heart and finally stop. These guys, in turn, make promises that they have no intention of keeping, such as they will sober up when they have kids or a better, less stressful job. No. There is no better time than the present.

Sometimes, all the love you can give will not be enough. Loving and dating someone with an addiction can eat up your soul. Letting go of a man you deeply love might seem unthinkable, but it's okay. At the end of the day, your peace of mind is a necessity and your responsibility.

**DON'T**
DATE HIM

**4**

## Don't Date Him If He Hogs the Driver's Seat. (Abusers)

Don't date him if he has low self-esteem.

Watch out for someone with low self-esteem. He could be six-foot-tall, have well-chiseled abs, and he could be in a profession that entails helping people, but he could be a man with low self-esteem. Unless you know a man closely, it would be difficult for you to understand he is a man with low self-esteem.

There are many causes of low self-esteem in men, from their issues with body image to reasons as varied as erectile dysfunction, toxic parenting, low levels of education or skills, and a sense of security.

A guy with such an attitude will enjoy putting you down to make themselves seem more important and have a misplaced sense of superiority or an inflated ego. Now, you don't want someone to be over-confident either. They also appear to misjudge how important they are. I always find it helpful to remind this type of guy how quickly he can be replaced by dumping them.

Some guys (as well as girls) with low self-esteem tend to be suspicious, insecure, and flirts. This, of course, can be very hurtful to you. They want their cake and want to screw it too.

Dating an overly suspicious man can be challenging. You could go to the next-door neighbor to get a match box, and he could think that he is hitting on you. You might return late from work, and he would think you were frolicking with your male co-workers. Because he has serious trust issues, don't be surprised if his mind is already made up on dumping you.

His low self-esteem would also make him unaware of healthy relationship boundaries. So, when you try to create some emotional boundaries, you will be met with some high-level resistance. Because you are already involved with him, and you love him, you will really need to tread carefully to handle his temper.

The fact that he is overly suspicious doesn't mean he may not be flirting with others. His grip on his woman doesn't in any way deter him from giving other women his attention.

He cheats because he constantly needs validation that he is desirable and charismatic. This is a massive downside of having a man with low self-esteem in your life. While he would want you to be exclusive, he wouldn't bat an eyelid before flirting with ladies at the party.

You should make a choice to value yourself enough not to let him tear you down. Men and women who don't cheat can be confident in knowing they have set a high standard for themselves. They are just looking for someone to behave in the same manner.

## Don't date him if he is hypersensitive. (See low self-esteem)

Hypersensitive, highly sensitive people or HSPs experience life and their relationships on an amplified level. Understanding a regular person is quite some work. Because hypersensitive people crave deep connections, being with them is challenging and is twice the work.

Hypersensitivity is a lot like hypochondria, and the feelings of people with this personality trait always get hurt. They are the romantics and overthinkers. As a result of their tendency to quickly pick up on things, they may see the threatening consequences of their partners' behaviors, reflect more, and worry about how things are going. Not everyone is willing to commit to this long-term work – managing an HSPs emotion.

Often enough, this is a cry for wholeness, something that you can never give another person. One must be OK with himself and with God. Only God can fill the void that we all will search for eventually.

## Don't date him if he hogs your driver's seat.

The hip-hop group TLC gave the perfect example of who this person is: S-C-R-U-B. Spotting a scrub isn't an arduous task. A scrub is someone who can't earn anything on his own, so they like to use yours. They give the appearance of being successful by living off your accomplishment and earnings. This person uses people for what they have because he is too darn lazy to earn it himself.

As women, we are approached by men almost every day. By putting their best foot forward, they may have tricked us into believing that they aren't scrubs; with time, their true colors eventually bleed through.

We all go through different phases when we attract losers, make mistakes by dating and getting engaged with them – this isn't a big deal. No one is exempt from making the occasional bad choice. But, for some weird reason, some women want to keep up with this trend.

**Does the guy you date spend most of his time talking about the big things he wants to do with his life but remains on his butt?**

You can't blame a man for having dreams, but there's nothing more frustrating and mentally draining than listening to him talk about things he is never going to do.

Yes, we all want to be wealthy, we all want to be admired for our achievements, and we all want to be appreciated by our fans and loved ones – but some of us don't get to be all of that.

We may have to sit at a desk all day, working at a 9-5 to get a promotion or pay rise after seven years. If the man in your life thinks he's bigger than all this and still does nothing to improve his financial situation, that's a very bad sign.

Do you always pay the bills? Does he owe you money all the time? How many soft loans have you given to him? How many of these loans has he paid? When was the last time he helped you financially? Is money a two-way street in your relationship?

**Does he move around with your car trying to hit up girls?**

If this is something your man does, he should absolutely be canceled. This doesn't have anything to do with the fact he hasn't got his own car.

Hollering at women on the street is sexist, absolutely disgusting, and a no-no.

The time to dump him was yesterday.

The next issue with this has to do with control. There has forever been a stereotype of men driving while women sit quietly in the passenger seat. When I was married, I preferred my husband to drive most of the time. I liked being chauffeured. However, when you're married, you're supposed to share everything except for the last Dr. Pepper; that is all mine.

## Don't date him if his father beat his mother or his children.

We all get angry from time to time. Being able to control your anger healthily will keep you out of trouble. The cycle of abuse is something that can be hard to break, but it can be smashed. For someone who has been exposed to a significant amount of violence, it can become a part of who they are, without them realizing it. Be very wary of someone who has suffered at the hands of an abuser. It is not easy to break the hold it can have over your life. If you had a parent who was an abuser, forgive them. Make darn sure you don't marry someone like them.

Break the cycle.

Men tend to take after their father. This means that someone tends to have similar traits as their parents. It is imperative to visit the man's home when still in the process of dating. This will allow you to interact with the family members, especially the father. A woman who is seriously looking for a man who has the qualities of a good husband should visit his family home to find out how he was raised. A wise woman should ask the neighbors about the history of the man's family, allowing her to make a wise decision about the future of the relationship.

## Don't date him if he tries to get you pregnant against your will.

When hunters see what they want, they will go after it. You hear stories of young girls doing this all the time. They find themselves in love with a boy and hope that the boy will magically fall in love by getting pregnant. She hopes this man will never leave her if she gives birth to his spawn. This often backfires, and the young girl finds herself subject to years of struggling, loneliness, and warfare due to raising a child on her own.

On the flip side, sometimes, a man of poor judgment will do the same thing in an attempt to keep the woman he wants. This type of man wants to keep these women at home barefoot, pregnant, and completely dependent on him. She will spend her life raising children, suffering at the hands of a control freak. She believes she can't leave because she will never be able to support her children and herself. She is trapped.

Women, get your education! Then if you want to stay with the control freak, it is your choice and not by the fear of having to make it on your own.

If you have chosen to abstain from sex until you are married, don't change your mind for fear of losing a man who is self-centered. If he truly loves you, he will help you stick to your decision.

It's a terrible warning sign when a man sees you as a sex object and is obsessed with getting you pregnant. Let's be honest, sex and pregnancy are just some of the many parts of a healthy and successful relationship. If these are his motivations, your relationship will lack depth, and you'll be hurt in the end.

## Don't date him if "no" is not in his vocabulary.

If you are a teenage girl and you are not ready to go further than a kiss. Then you are not ready, and that should be respected. Once you give into something you are not ready for, it can sometimes lead you to feelings of regret.

A guy needs to understand that "NO" means "NO". A guy trying to force you to do something you don't want is not the right fellow. If a man cares for you, he understands that everything needs to be perfect for both of you. The perfect dude wants everything to work out between the two of you.

The precise timing will be central to both of you. A guy that keeps trying to force himself on you is not in it for the both of you. He's in it for his pecker.

## Don't date him if he has ever threatened to kill himself over someone he has dated.

Another way people can sometimes try to control others is by threatening to harm themselves. As someone with a degree in counseling, I have an obligation to report threats of self-harm, harm to children, the elderly, and the disabled. On the other hand, I have seen people say, "I will kill myself if you leave me." To this, I reply, "Go ahead." He then moved on to his next tactic of trying to keep me. I knew he liked himself too much to kill himself. If you are genuinely afraid for your life or the life of another, however, call the authorities immediately. This will keep your conscience clear, knowing you helped. After you've done that, leave him alone entirely, move, and change numbers because this is not the type of person you want to get involved with.

A woman should be careful with the category of men that she deals with. A woman should keep far away from people that threaten to kill themselves for any reason. Such people can threaten to kill themselves if you refuse their proposal, or they might threaten you as a condition to do what they want.

Gentlemen do not threaten to kill themselves, and you know them through their behaviors. When dating, it is advisable to avoid this type of man to save yourself from problems.

## Don't date him if he keeps on giving you ultimatums.

"If you do not do this, I am going to…"

Men who give ultimatums to women they claim to love do not love them. Women who find themselves with such men should realize that this is supposed to be a personal relationship, not a professional one.

Ultimatums and deadlines are given to employees, not to life partners. No ultimatums or heads-up required. However, on the contrary, sometimes a stipulation may need to be given for a person to make a choice for the betterment of the relationship. For example, if your significant other finds it necessary to start smoking around you. Whether you are a guy or a girl, for own personal health reasons, an ultimatum can be given to save the health of your own body. If you give an ultimatum, you stick to it.

## Don't date him if he belittles your interests.

Your interests and your hobbies are what make you special and unique. Whether it's because of their own insecurity or jealousy, sometimes you meet people who disapprove of the things you like. For example, if you love dressing up and consider makeup as a form of art, but the guy you are dating contemplates "going natural" to be better, then you need to see if there is a happy median. You need to feel good, but he wants you to look a certain way.

When your interests are being sidelined, it can feel like you're being kicked in the gut. It becomes worse when your partner is the one doing it. No one deserves such lousy behavior from someone they love.

Unless you are doing something harmful, do not listen to any guy who asks you to give up on your interests just because he does not like them.

## Don't date him if he does not make you feel beautiful.

It's understandable that self-confidence and self-esteem are not things everyone can switch on when they wake up. Just because you feel something or you're told something doesn't mean it is true.

To a man who truly loves you, you are not ugly. Be with someone who makes you feel beautiful, even if you don't think you are. At some point in our lives, we all feel insecure, despite being told our image of ourselves is wrong.

You are beautiful and special, so if you feel someone finds you ugly, they are not the right person for you. Don't judge your beauty by what you think someone is thinking.

Strive for a man that builds you up, despite your insecurities, because you deserve the best.

## Don't Date Him If You Are the Fourth Person He Calls When He Has Good News. (Priorities)

You know how important you are by how important people make you feel. If no one thinks you're important, you'll know. If a guy cares about you, he thinks of you at the top of his list. If a man cares for you, he initiates communication via phone call or email. He also initiates communication by texting or using an instant message. It is important for both parties in a relationship to make an effort to contact each other. When he has good news, he calls you first instead of his friends and makes you a priority. For example, my ex-husband would rather avoid talking on the telephone unless he liked the person. Hence, it is important to ensure there is contact both ways in a relationship. Otherwise, this is a one-way highway that you need to exit.

## Don't date him if he disappears for 24 hours at a time.

My ex-husband was the king of disappearing. One time, I fell asleep on the couch, and he disappeared out of the bedroom window. I guess he wanted to go out.

There are various reasons why men disappear. Men vanish because something about their woman does not fit into their perception of a relationship. Men don't like staying with the ladies who are too needy and dependent before they are ready. Also, men do not like remaining with the girls who are controlling. It's a fine line we women must walk. People disappear because women are not able to meet their needs or do not know how to determine their partner's needs. Priority is important in any relationship. Men and women should make their partners a priority in life to prevent him or her from disappearing. On the other hand, jerks may disappear for 24 hours or more at a time because they are cheating, and in that case, it is time for you to disappear too.

## Don't date him if he makes you miserable when the two of you do something he doesn't want to do.

This is a classic case of selfishness. There are some people who, if they don't get their way, will make you highly miserable in your quest to have fun. Relationships are about compromise.

When you love someone, you are supposed to take turns enjoying what the other person wants. Some guys and girls will sabotage a new adventure time because they are selfish. If someone is not violating your standards as to who you are, don't piss on their parade; you wouldn't want someone to crap on yours. Being selfish affects relationships and makes it difficult for partners to enjoy each other's company. For instance, my friend, Amy, was selfish in her first college relationship. She stated, "I always wanted to have my way to be happy. I always pestered my man to have enough time with him. Though he spent time with me on weekends, I was not satisfied and wanted to be with him during weekdays. This affected our relationship badly, and our relationship ended. He never violated my standards as to who I was, and I was not supposed to be jealous."

## Don't date him if he gets a card and gives it to you while it's still in the bag.

The kind of gifts a man gives is an indicator of how important you are to him. Men who see their women as important parts of their lives pleasantly give them gifts. For instance, they ensure the card is signed and put in an envelope. Also, they put different kinds of gifts inside the envelope, like jewelry. Also, they take their women out for a romantic dinner from time to time. On the other hand, men who see their woman as less of a priority give them weird gifts. For example, they give their woman gifts that are not wrapped and do not have any form of authentication like a signature in the case of a card. In most cases, such men do not see their partners (wives) as important parts of their lives. These are filler girls or a friend with benefits. Men do not have a serious relationship with friends with benefits and do not see them as important in their lives. They only get involved with them for fun or out of loneliness but do not make serious commitments to them. Although they may like these women, there is something that does not inspire them to make the filler girls their girlfriends. They only use them until they find the right partner. Never become a filler girl. Always wait to become the sweetheart. This is a girl that a man adores and can't wait to see. Something in this woman inspires him to claim her as his partner. Hence, if your man gives you a card that is not put in an envelope, then he may not appreciate you. I had a friend once whose husband gave her a card in a bag for Valentine's Day. The card was not signed, not in an envelope, and there weren't any other gifts. Oddly enough, things got ugly when she found out that her husband gave his girlfriend a nice romantic dinner and jewelry.

## Don't date him if he goes out without you.

Let me further clarify this: I am not talking about the occasional night out with the boys. When I say this, I am speaking about a man who leaves his pregnant wife at home so he can go hoeing. You deserve so much more than that. If he doesn't come home, trust me, someone would love to be there with you. He doesn't deserve you, and you aren't a priority in his life. Ladies should inform their men that they want to be involved and occasionally go out on actual dates. People should be willing to provide it, and women should not be scared to ask for it.

## Don't date him if he does not want to introduce you to his friends and family.

Men don't just bring up any woman to their buddies. If he talks about you, it's because he likes you and his friends should get to know your name. If a man talks about you with his friends and introduces you to the people in his life, then it means he likes you. Here is a secret: the more taken he is with you, the quicker he wants you to meet his mother. Pass the parent test, and you've just won an award. If he doesn't introduce you to anyone, it is important to figure out why. Is he embarrassed by his friends? Is he embarrassed by you? Or does he think there is no point for the people he loves to bother remembering your name?

## Don't date him if he has already had three other girlfriends this year.

A man's seriousness in relationships is determined by the kind of relationships he has been in and how often he has dumped his girlfriends. People who are committed and thoughtful when dating tend to have long-lasting relationships, love, and care for their partners. They also know their partners are a priority in their lives and respect them. A man is not serious and committed if he has had three girlfriends or relationships in a year. A fickle person is annoying. If he is going through women like toilet paper, someone is bound to get hurt and rest assured, it won't be him. Now understand, dating is one term, but a 'girlfriend' or 'boyfriend' title comes with a certain type of commitment. It should mean, "We like each other, so let's give it some time to see where we want it to go." To call someone your girlfriend means you're special. If he has already called someone his girlfriend three times this year, how special are you?

I say this for many reasons. First, a person should take their time once they have "broken up" with their partner. It is important that if you have just been through a bad relationship, you spend some time on your own. Figure out how your ex has made an impact on you for the worse and then repair the damage rather than dragging the emotional luggage with you into your next relationship.

People who jump from one relationship to another do not give themselves enough time to reflect on the reasons that it could not work between them and their ex. Some reflection is important if you ultimately want to settle down into a healthy, loving relationship.

## Don't date him if he doesn't follow through with his plans.

My friend, Annie, was dating a guy who had a bad habit of canceling at the last minute. We understand when something important came up at work, and hence, you cannot meet us for the coffee date you promised us, but ditching us four times in a row?

Yeah, that's not happening.

When a guy is continually canceling his plans with you, it just means this: you are not important. Other things are important, and you just do not happen to be top of the list. At this point, the best hope you can have is to get out while you still can, with your dignity intact.

Remember Annie? Well, at the beginning of their relationship, her boyfriend never canceled on her, and he always showed up on time. Once he got the idea that Annie was hooked, then he started slacking. Annie was not having any of it and cut him loose; after the third time, he "overslept."

## Don't date him if he substitutes his actual presence with gifts.

Nobody dislikes gifts, they are necessary for healthy relationships, but there are men who prefer to give you gifts instead of giving you their attention and time.

While getting stuffed animals and gold jewelry is lovely, too, it does not make up for the actual connection that can only be built with time and thought. Although it may sound ridiculous that I am advocating to be wary of a guy who gives you all the gifts you want, I promise it will not be funny after being in a relationship with such a man. Women, above everything else, want to be heard, so while the watch he just sent you may be expensive, it will not listen to you.

Quality time and attention are some of the most special gifts ever. If your relationship is based on objects alone, it's not much more than a series of transactions. Gifts will fade, but memories will last. A man who is invested in creating beautiful memories with you by giving you the attention you deserve should be treasured.

## Don't date a workaholic.

Guys with no ambitions are a turn-off, but guys who are too far on the other side of the scale should quickly turn you off too. If his commitment to work is more than his commitment to you, then it is evident that you are not a priority in his life. Time management skills are sometimes lacking in men. Date men who know how to utilize their time and manage to both meet their deadlines and keep their relationships.

I met a lady some years ago who had been seeing a guy for a month. Her attraction toward him was strong early on, and he was the perfect man for her on every level.

The first three weeks were beautiful, and he used every available opportunity to keep in touch with her. After each date, she would get a text message within hours. On other occasions, he would send random ones in the morning wishing her a great day. They saw each other twice a week until he had to leave the country for business. While away, they kept in touch via text messages.

When he got back, he bought her a new phone and a text message saying he missed her and would get a hold of her over the weekend. Everything seemed back to normal, but he didn't make good his promise.

She was really worried, so she called and left a message on Monday.

The silence went on for three days, and all she got was a text saying he was still working. The few times they talked, he avoided discussing spending time with her. This pattern continued for two weeks until she called him up, telling him that she realized that he would not give her the attention she needed with his schedule.

He didn't bother trying to convince her otherwise. He was honest with her and told her he didn't want to make promises he couldn't keep. At this point, it was too late. She needed to be happy in their relationship, but he couldn't give that to her.

She asked me whether I thought she did the right thing.

I told her a man who loves her should desire to see her, especially when he just returned from an international trip. The fact that he didn't implies that he wasn't as crazy about her as she was about him. This doesn't mean the relationship couldn't grow into that stage.

It was still budding for him, and he chose other things before her.

Having said that, you must do what you believe is best for you when the man in your life is a workaholic.

## Don't date him if he confides more in his friends than in you.

Good relationships are all about trust. We share secrets, our problems, and our concerns with people who are not just close to our hearts but also who we can trust.

Your boyfriend can and should have close friends other than you, but if he turns to his friends every time he has something bothering him, then that is a red flag. It could potentially mean that he does not trust you. He might try to rationalize it by saying that his "guys" understand him, which may be true, but if he is in a relationship, it is important to understand your place in his support system.

We live in strange times where anything goes, especially in relationships. Your man should trust you and love you enough to confide in you above anyone else. If this is a hard task, it shows that there is something wrong somewhere.

If you can't be very good friends with him, why should you date him? If he prefers confiding in his friends and not you, or you constantly get wind of certain bits of information from his friends because he bypassed you, you shouldn't date him.

This is a clear show of disrespect and lack of trust in you.

## Don't date him if he always "forgets" that one thing you told him to do.

You have been asking your guy for something that he has been very casually "forgetting." In other words, this translates into the fact that he does not consider you a priority.

When you matter to someone, you don't forget what they had asked you to do. It all boils down to how important you consider them.

It's understandable that the human brain can overload itself. A man who casually and constantly forgets things you discussed doesn't take you seriously.

If this is the usual trend and it's something you have addressed before, you shouldn't bother with him. This behavior shows what is coming your way in the future.

Immediately cut him off; he is not worth your time and day. Forget about him and move on.

**DON'T**
DATE HIM

**6**

## Don't Date Him If He Brings You Lingerie that Looks Used. (Other women)

> Don't date him if he brings you
> lingerie that looks used.

My roommate's story is enough to exhibit why this is an important message. Alyssa, my roommate, and I decided to go out with a couple of guys we met at our favorite club. The guys seemed pretty nice, and after a while, the fella that was seeing Alyssa brought her a bag of lingerie. We assumed it was his way of saying he wanted to take their relationship to the next level. We were wrong.

We pulled her gift out of the bag and what we

immediately noticed was how large the lingerie was – it had to be about eight sizes too large for tiny Alyssa. Then, we saw something disgusting: there were several large stains on the panties. Horrified, Alyssa threw everything in the trash. Alyssa and I asked around the club, and apparently, the man had a rather large wife. Not only was this man two-timing his wife and Alyssa, but he was also too cheap to buy her new lingerie! He was trying to get credit from two women for a single gift. He and his friend, guilty by association, never again heard from Alyssa or myself. Beware of the man who brings you used clothes!

> Don't date him if his eyes wander to other women while he is on a date with you.

Men should appreciate their partner's beauty. A man who loves his girlfriend does not keep staring at other women and undermining his partner. These behaviors can lead to low self-esteem and little general confidence. Guys who are serious about their partners accept the way they are and respect them. Why I would date such idiots, I don't know, but I once dated this guy who would always stare at other girls when we were together.

He would walk past a girl and would turn around and gawk. When a man treats you this way, it is meant to demean who you are. Find someone who only has eyes for you, regardless of whether you're present or not.

## Don't date him if he is already in a relationship with someone else.

Pet peeve! Rant alert! I will try to be as gentle as I can. I understand a woman craving a challenge, and the need to win without any consequences can be intoxicating. However, there are always consequences from taking something that doesn't belong to you. Maybe he told you he is unhappy and intends to leave his wife, but take heed; if this is true, he will leave his wife rather than making you the other woman. Walk a mile in the other woman's shoes. How would you feel if you found out your partner had someone on the side? Furthermore, I don't think God will ever tell a woman to date another woman's husband. I know a woman who has been wedged in this trap for six years. She will never honestly be happy because she knows he will be returning to his wife at the end of each day. If you need a challenge, try taking care of yourself first. Figure out what you need in a companion. Faithfulness should be at the top of the list.

Also, if you are attracted to someone who you know is committed to someone else, do not lie to yourself by trying to convince yourself that "he is just a friend" or "he is just a crush" and continue spending time with him. You may not have confessed it to him, but you know it in your heart that you are crossing a line.

Although it may be difficult, the adult thing to do here would be to keep a healthy distance between yourself and this man. A healthy range here does not just mean turning a corner every time you see him walking towards you, but limiting all contact and keeping strict boundaries.

## Don't date him if he has two cell phones.

Signs that show that a man is cheating on his wife or girlfriend can be found. You will have to learn to obverse behavior. Jerks who are cheating on their wives or girlfriends have more than two cells phones. One of the cell phones is for the wife or girlfriend, and the other is for the other woman. These men are sly and make it difficult for each woman to find out about the other, and women need to be aware of the deeper meaning of their actions. Similarly, he may make excuses not to answer his phone when he is with you or, contrary, take hours or days to return your phone calls. I once knew a guy that carried two cell phones. One of them would ring, and a voice could be heard, "Where you at? Where you at?" We always knew that was his wife. The other phone was his throw-away phone. Always question throw-away phones. Yes, companies do issue cell phones, but usually, it is apparent if it is a work phone or a personal phone. Remember, a wife can call on any phone. A girlfriend on the side has a particular phone.

## Don't date him if he can't answer his phone in front of you.

As mentioned above, men who are playing the field will not answer their phones in front of you because it could be another woman. When in doubt, just listen to Destiny's Child. "Say my name, say my name." If he can't answer phone calls in front of you and won't say your name when he does respond to the phone, take it as a sign he doesn't want you to hear.

## Don't date him if he says she's just his friend or his cousin.

I do have old male friends. We still call each other best

friends from time to time because we were both once road dogs when we were young. I was black, and he thought he was black.

Perfect friendship. We were always up to many shenanigans. As we grew up, we could no longer hang out the way we used to. It was now inappropriate for us to be married to other people and run the streets with each other. Although we may hook up with our families together, we know there is a certain respect that we must have for our spouses, and we would never want our friendship ever to look dishonest.

Now, to my point, my other point.

## Don't date him if he is still online dating.

Many men continue to have active online dating accounts while they are dating for many reasons. Firstly, they do not love their current partners and want to play the dating field. Secondly, men have active online dating accounts because they feel insecure. Such people believe that their relationships will not work out and hence need to continue searching for backup partners. Open communication is necessary from the beginning. If you two are going out on your first date, ask him how many people he is currently seeing. This is important to know so that you can understand the relationship and the boundaries. Many men use the online dating scene as a "booty- call- gone- lazy service" and hence disappoint their partners by cheating on them. Mary discovered that her boyfriend was cheating on her as he had an active online dating account and communicated with his other girlfriends, often using the account. After asking her boyfriend about the account, he said he had prepaid the account for a year. At first, she listened to his story, but after examining the account, she noticed that her boyfriend was sending emails to his other girlfriends. If you discover that your boyfriend has an online dating account, dump him. Dumping him will prevent you from being hurt in the future.

## Don't date him if he won't make it exclusive to you.

You have been dating someone for quite a long time, and it is obvious that the two of you like each other, but despite this, it is still not exclusive. Despite telling you that he has feelings for you, he does not want to make your relationship an "exclusive" affair, so you need to stop dating him immediately.

Yeah, what's the need to keep up with the charade when you want and deserve better? Beyond the feelings, if he truly loves you, he wouldn't find making the commitment a difficult one.

Otherwise, you will continue falling deeper in love with this person. As you are waiting, time passes, and you are crushed when the relationship inevitably fails. He was being very honest with you because you were not it and was keeping his options open.

## Don't date him if he is cheating on his girlfriend with you.

I know I have already gone through this. Just because he isn't married does not mean it's OK for you to see him while he is currently in a voiced relationship with someone else. You need to set your standards as high as you want them. He cannot be trusted if he sees someone outside when he is supposed to be in a committed relationship. You should let him know you are worthy and must be respected.

Women should not date a man who is cheating on his girlfriend with them as he will do the same to them. He will drop them as soon as he finds someone else, and they will end up getting disappointed. Continuing to date him when you know he has a girlfriend is not okay as it will hurt his girlfriend badly. Also, you do not want this to happen to you in the future, so you should avoid seeing him because he is not faithful, committed, and trustworthy. Also, he does not respect and love his girlfriend; otherwise, he would not be cheating.

## Don't date him if he still stalks his exes.

You met a perfect guy, and you begin dating. The more you know about him, the more you find yourself attracted to him.

Unfortunately, you notice one little thing: he seems to mention his ex A LOT. He is either not over her, or he still has feelings for her. It is a psychological fact that if you are truly over someone, you do not speak about them or stalk them! If there are truly no feelings left, then there would be no thought or energy to figure out what their ex is doing in life.

You probably also made a decision to stop seeing someone you once dated to be with this guy. Why then should someone in their right senses stalk a person they decided to break up with?

"Ex-stalkers" are typically still interested in that ex. He never got over the break-up, so he is still carrying the baggage from that relationship.

Do you know that a stalker is an abuser? In the mind of a stalker, his ex is someone who had no right to leave him. This attitude already shows you what he thinks about his girlfriends – items he owns and has no right to leave him. There's a good chance he will do the same thing to you.

Sensible men know how sensitive the subject of exes can be and know to avoid this topic altogether.

## Don't date him if he constantly compares you with the other women in his life.

No two people are the same, and that is what makes everyone so unique. You have your own set of strengths and weaknesses, just as other women have their strengths and weaknesses.

Beware of men who continuously remind you of how the other women in his life treat him, how they do everything for him, and how they never say no to his requests.

If he does this, he clearly doesn't rate or appreciate you. Such a guy is not good enough for you. Comparing you with other women borders on emotional abuse and shouldn't be condoned.

Good guys understand that every person, irrespective of their gender, in their life has their place; hence drawing comparisons between people is ridiculous, childish, and unfair.

## Don't Date Him If He Believes that All Men Find Other Men Attractive Sometimes

Yeah, I know; as I said before, I have been on the world's worst dates. Back in the 90s, I happened to be dating a guy who showed a unique interest in my make-up. I offered to put make-up on him, and he replied, "You can put make-up on me. I don't care." That was my first clue. I ignored it. A couple of weeks later, we were having a casual conversation about the differences between men and women. He stated that every man finds other men attractive. We soon stopped dating, and one year later, I heard he was a self-proclaimed bisexual male. About ten years later, I dated another man who offered to take me to a gay bar (on the premise that his cousin worked there). I then decided to ask him the same question I asked my ex. "Do you think all men find other men attractive?" He said, "Yes" and I never saw him again. Let me say this once; if someone is gay, that is their business, but it is not fair to date someone when they can never fulfill your needs. And honey, you cannot fulfill a gay guy's needs.

## Don't date him if he has weird fetishes you are not comfortable with.

Some fetishes may be fun to indulge in, but if the guy you are dating is into overly kinky and borderline dangerous/harmful acts, you need to escape while you still can. It is important to be with someone that will make you feel contented.

Once I dated a guy that always wanted to role play during sex. It was never just him and me; it was always some crazy scenario. I finally had to conclude that he had some real issues.

I knew that I would never be able to satisfy him on a personal level. He was always looking for a fantasy that would lend him to a lifetime prison sentence if it came true. Eventually, it just sickened me, and I stopped dating him.

DON'T
DATE HIM

8

## Don't Date Him If You Haven't Run a Credit Check. (Money)

> Don't date him if you haven't run a credit check.

Women should be well aware of who and what they are marrying before they take their final vows. For instance, there would be nothing worse than getting married, picturing your beautiful home with a white picket fence, and then finding out that your husband's credit is so bad that you can't even get approved for a loan on a bar of soap, let alone a house. Reality check, ladies: when you get married, have a clear picture of his credit score and what taking on his name means! Your debt is now his, and vice versa.

If your man has no credit, that is not necessarily a negative quality. It gives you room to grow. However, if his credit is bad, that is a whole different story. Not only will there be no SUV to drive your children to and from school if you ever get divorced, but you may also end up with at least half his problems. If you decide to marry a man who has debt, it is your responsibility to ask those tough questions and make sure you are ready to carry all that he carries. If he has been honest with you and is working to improve his credit, this is a positive sign. Remember, it takes seven years to remove negative items on a credit report; judgments and fore-closures can remain on the report for much longer.

Maybe you think this isn't serious or that it doesn't apply to you. You're young, he's young, and you ask yourself about how bad it can be? Let me tell you a quick story. One of my friend's husbands died unex-pectedly. During her grief, she found out that he had been leading a double life. His job had required a lot of travel, or so she thought, and while he was away from her home in Houston, he had set up another home, complete with a wife and children, in California. He would spend a few weeks in Texas and then a few weeks in California, claiming it was necessary for work. His unexpected death left her with $40,000 of debt, much of which funded his other family in California.

Since he had made the purchases using their joint

accounts, she was now responsible for paying for the other woman's furniture, clothes, etc. Everyone is entitled to one free credit report each year. A quick check now can mean skipping a lot of problems later... just ask my friend!

## Don't date him until you've done a criminal background check.

If you thought the credit check was crazy, you must think I am completely nuts recommending a criminal background check. Although this is a good idea for any woman, this is necessary if you are a single parent. Could you forgive yourself if you found out that the good-looking, child-loving, outgoing man who has been so friendly with your kids is a convicted child molester?

You know you have read these stories in the newspapers, and if you looked at the pictures, the guys could be anyone.

I had a friend, we'll call her Sarah, and Sarah's boyfriend would sometimes act a little odd. This guy was very handsome, but he was extremely closed off when she would try to ask him about himself. She thought it was odd, and I did too, and I recommended a background check.

Sarah called me in a panic several days later. She had taken my advice and had a friend who was a local officer run a region search for his name. I had expected a drug possession charge or something similar, but no, that was not the case. The guy she was dating was arrested in Africa for molestation accusations of a child. The charges were dropped against him there. However, I have never been one to be speechless, but after hearing that, I was at a complete loss for words.

On a less serious note, but still, on this topic, I dated a guy once, long before I was smart enough to run background checks. I assumed the best of him, as is the tendency of most young women, and was surprised that we were not approved for a single decent apartment when we applied together. The only place that would take him was known for being a crack-selling complex. Not surprisingly, he had a hard time finding employment as well – those background checks can cause trouble for someone who has a messy background!

His problems become your problems when you decide to date him. If you knowingly accept his problems, that is your choice, but empower yourself to make a good choice. Get all the information. If you don't know someone in law enforcement, ask around, and I'm positive you can find this information. If you can't find anyone, look online; many states now keep criminal records online and accessible to the public. Your significant other might not be happy that you have run a background check, but what does that say about them? Would you be offended if someone ran a background check on you before letting you into their lives? The only reason to be seriously offended is if you have something to hide, in which case you are only trying to transfer the blame. Let's face it: everyone makes mistakes. A decent person would own up to them. It's an opportunity to show the person you want to date that you have changed. It is crucial to find these things out before you fall in love. Once you fall in love, it takes a long time to fall out of love.

## Don't date him if he wants you to pick up the tab.

I have learned to be a firm believer in "no money, no honey." Keep in mind this does not apply to college students because we all have times of struggle. I have dated a couple of guys who seek out women who are doing it on their own. These men have no desire to better themselves; their whole mission in life is to live off someone else. When you can't give in to their greedy wants anymore, they will find someone else to take care of them.

This is the catcher, though; when they truly fall

in love, they will finally try to improve themselves. I will tell for free that this is a line used by some of the world's biggest losers.

You should also be wary of this line: He says, "I'm hungry." You say, "I'm starving, too. Let's go get something to eat." He says, "I don't have any money." Run; because he is out to drain you dry. He knows that you have cash, and he wants you to pick up the tab. Give him the cash and watch him spend it!

Guys who never offer to pay are not gentlemen; there are basically freeloaders. If you continue paying the bills, you are enabling him to think that his behavior is acceptable. If he tried it with you, rest assured that he has done it in the past.

No one has an entitlement to receive and take without reciprocating goodwill. Avoid men with such mindsets and appreciate the ones who treat you well.

## Don't date him if you are a huge money spender, and he is too.

Money is one of the main causes of conflicts in marriage and relationships and even leads to broken homes if couples are unable to resolve their differences. This is one reason why opposites attract, to help balance out a relationship. Two big spenders equal a whole lot of arguments over money. One of you will always miss out because the other partner is buying what they want first. Also, money has made it hard for partners to trust each other and negatively affected their relationships.

Sheen and her husband, Sam, have been married for nine years and have had a major problem with spending. Sheen's man was full of nasty financial surprises. Like having over a hundred thousand dollars in student loans.

However, Sam put their honeymoon on her emergency credit card, forcing Sheen to pay the debt. Sam did not inform her about the debt until it was too late. A few weeks later, Sam used Sheen's company's credit card, and this led to a huge fight between him and his wife. They continue to experience problems as Sam mismanages the family money.

## Don't date him if he tries to control your money.

Women should not date men who control them in any aspect. No human has the right to control another human. A man who loves his wife must trust her and not control her finances because he knows his wife is responsible enough and capable. Men who aggressively control their women are losers. Controlling a woman's finances is another sign of an abuser.

This person will make sure you are completely dependent on him. He will attempt to make sure you will never be self-sufficient enough to do anything on your own. This is his way of keeping you under his feet.

Financial independence is a highly important matter for a lot of women. This is also one of the reasons why most women choose to remain working even after having settled down with the right man. The right man, in this case, is not only supportive of this woman's ambitious nature, but he would also not try to dictate where she can and cannot spend the money. He considers her wise and mature enough to make these decisions on her own.

## Don't date him if he asks to borrow money.

A male gold digger makes my stomach turn. They love to take advantage of women trying to do something for themselves.

A lady once asked me if she should keep giving money to her boyfriend of 7 years; he had been borrowing money from her all this time.

This is what I told her, "If he repays his debt in full in a timely manner, this is fine. At least your money isn't disappearing into an abyss of greed and neediness. It's still worrisome that he is always asking you for money. How can you tell that he truly loves you or if he only hangs around you because he sees you as Ms. Moneybags? Irrespective of how difficult things may have been for him, after 7 years, a man should be out of the cycle of borrowing from his girlfriend or other people. What exactly does he use this borrowed money for? Is he purchasing items he wants but doesn't need?"

Beyond all of this, the fact that a man makes a habit of borrowing shows that he is not dependable. Unintentionally becoming his crutch is a painful thing to go through because you genuinely want to help, but it ends up draining you emotionally and financially.

Single mothers, I speak to you: be careful! It's a terrible business to get entangled with a man who is not financially stable. These men like to target someone looking for stability. No one has the right to use you or your earnings without your knowledge.

A man should make decisions responsibly, and that also includes financial decisions. Your role in his life is not to always bail him out of his financial quandary every time he messes up. A good man should have some pride and be able to meet his basic needs.

If you have a delinquent borrower in your life, be grateful you aren't married to him. Find ways to completely cut him off. He is the least of your worries.

**DON'T**
DATE HIM

**9**

# Don't Date Him If His Expectations of You Seem Crazy.
# (His Respect Issues)

People have different expectations when they start dating. Men and women expect their significant other to behave in a certain manner. Setting expectations in a relationship are important at the very beginning. This will help to avoid conflicts and make their relationship a success. However, setting the wrong expectations or crazy expectations can negatively affect the relationship. Women should not date men who have crazy expectations because one person will be expecting more than the other, and hence you will not be comfortable as you try to meet these false hopes.

## Don't date him if he makes any comments, even joking comments, about your body or weight.

Men and women should accept each other for the way they are, instead of making fun comments about their partner's body and weight. For instance, if a man is dating a larger lady, he should not make rude comments about her, which could affect her self-esteem and relationship.

Many, many years ago, when I was a size 4, I had a date with this guy who I thought was "hot." We met at my favorite club, and I strutted over to where he was standing. He pinched my nonexistent stomach and said, "You're fat." I immediately turned around and walked off without ever saying another word to him. Even in my 20s, I understood the importance of self-esteem and the inevitable need for some people to try to put you down was. The idea that someone would try to put me down, regardless of how I looked, was a sign of a bigger issue. I was not going to put myself in a situation where someone was going to say ugly things about me, especially while on our first date! Body image is a very sensitive topic. Body image activists tell you to accept and love your body before you can expect others to treat it with love and respect it so obviously deserves. I agree 100%, but in the real world, even if you are comfortable in your skin, there will be people who will put you down for it. In situations like these, know that you are beautiful regardless of what others have to say about it. Own your ground.

> Don't date him if he comments or jokes about other women's body or weight.

A person's character is the only thing that stands between them and greatness. It is also the only thing that is remembered after they die. I heard it said many times: "Character is who a person is when no one else is around."

We are all entitled to our own attractions, but body-shaming is toxic and unacceptable behavior. It has become rampant nowadays, with both men and women experiencing it. No matter the body shape, body size, and looks of a person, they shouldn't be judged based on their features or appearance.

When people hear cruel or negative comments about their body, the effect can be devastating and humiliating; it can go on to affect their self-esteem and lead to depression and eating disorders.

The guy you are dating may not have said anything to you about your appearance, but he is very vocal about stating his opinions on how other women around look. If this guy is putting women down behind their backs, he will eventually put you down to yours. I have seen women who could easily be Victoria's Secret models stuck with men who still find something to criticize.

There is no pleasing some people, I guess. Nobody should be made to feel ashamed by the way they look. Don't tolerate this attitude from the man you want to date or anyone else.

## Don't date him if he is too controlling.

Controlling men do not make for good partners. "Control" can start out mildly, with little things that may be easy to excuse away.

Pay attention because such men always start so small, asking you to change little things about yourself, and of course, you do it all in the name of love. These little things can build over time to become more extreme until he is completely dominant over you and the relationship. Before you know it, however, you have changed so much that you would not even recognize yourself.

Let me tell you the story of one of my friends which happened years ago. She met this handsome and generous guy. In the beginning, they toured different countries together. He showered her with love and gifts, treating her like a queen. Soon, she moved in with him.

The control started with the small things. He insisted that she put on certain outfits not necessarily because anything was wrong with them but because they were not his taste. He soon started getting upset that she had lunch with us – her friends every Friday; this made her stop hanging out with us unless he was included. Any plans she made, he reversed.

Eight months later, she called me excitedly to tell me he had bought her a car. I was delighted for her, so I asked, "When can we take it for a spin?" She hesitated and said, "I will need his permission to do that. I can't go anywhere with the car without his OK."

I was stunned, to say the least. I let her in on my thoughts. I told her the car was his car, and she should treat it that way.

Soon, the verbal abuse started. He told her she was weak and silly and made every decision that concerned them. Slowly but surely, she became a prisoner in their own apartment and a shadow of her bubbly self.

It is one thing to listen to what he needs and ways to compromise, but if he belittles your choices, your views, and your ways of life, he has got to go. If he is to stay, then he must accept you for who you are. And that includes everything, your good, your bad, and the ugly in between.

When a guy is controlling, have nothing to do with him. He will also be a controlling husband/dad.

## Don't date him if he puts you down in front of other people.

Someone who likes to embarrass you in public is a sure sign of an abuser. Belittling someone in front of people or behind closed doors is abusive.

I believe people who take joy in belittling other people suffer from a lack of self-esteem and self-love. They do it to make their victims look weak and themselves better and superior.

This abuse can begin as digs disguised as jokes. Your boyfriend may tease, ridicule, and humiliate you with sarcastic remarks about your appearance and abilities in front of your friends. They may laugh at his wisecracks, but you felt it, and your brain struggles to come to terms with his put-down.

If you show your displeasure, he may patronize you with, "You are too sensitive; I was only kidding." He maintains his nice guy façade, refuses to apologize, and those around may wonder why you are getting worked up over a mindless joke. His denial of your displeasure adds another layer to his abuse.

If you allow his ridicule and put-downs to continue, it will severely damage your self-esteem and integrity.

Men are supposed to respect and adore their partners, even when in front of other people. Women are to be revered and respected by the person they are dating. A man is supposed to protect his woman. It's in a man's DNA to seek out relationships that allow them to act like a protector. If he isn't protecting you, he isn't worth dating.

If he puts her down in front of friends and family, he will be the first to bail out when a crisis hits. A man who does not adore and respect his girlfriend or wife before all others does not love them and can abandon them in a crisis. Hence, women should dump a boyfriend if they notice that he does not respect and adore them regardless of who he is.

## Don't date him if he treats you differently in public.

Some men treat their women differently when they are in front of others and are entirely different person to them when in private. Decent guys treat their women with love and care, irrespective of where they are and who is presently in front of them.

A friend of mine was with a guy who was always so sweet to her when her friends and family were around. However, when she left him saying that he was abusive to her in private, it was complicated for her to convince others that she was stating the obvious truth. I remember many people from her circle telling her that she left him because she was ungrateful because he was a gem of a person. Why would anyone want to leave a guy who treats you *that* well?

People that were saying those things did not know what kind of a person he was behind closed doors.

## Don't date him if things start moving too fast, too soon.

Sometimes, it can feel impossible to win in the dating business because of a whole ton of clichés.

You will be labeled dramatic if you're expressive of your feelings. If you're upset when he cheats, you're termed intolerant. You're a cold fish if you manage a breakup with calmness.

Some men are famous for rushing into relationships, just as women are also guilty of moving too fast in a relationship. Most of the time, the fear of losing this person makes people jump too fast.

It's time to take a break and stop getting rushed into a relationship. The more you allow this, the harder it will be to find love.

Not all men are good, as some men like taking advantage of women. Such men exploit women financially and sexually. Love takes time. When you fail to invest real time and effort in a relationship, you may never learn what it feels like to love.

Women should take time before they start dating a man to know more about him and his intentions. Taking time to know a person better ensures that women are not disappointed in the future. It equally helps you see if you are a good match for each other. Love might find you tomorrow or in the next couple of years. Your friends and family love you; this should be enough. There is no crime in being single. So, enjoy your life. By taking things one step at a time, you might find that he loves you.

Another sign of an abuser is if he wants to jump into a relationship very quickly, without even getting to know a girl. This guy is usually looking for a free ride. Sometimes, they think they are praying for someone weak and needy.

## Don't date him if he will not stand up for you in front of others.

As mentioned earlier, men should protect their wives and defend them no matter the circumstance. However, most men are not able to do so because they are not confident enough to confront these challenges. Confidence in each other is something you need to have to make a relationship grow. You run into difficulties with this when your mother-in-law gets involved. You want to know your man has your back no matter what the circumstance, and he must understand that you come first.

Respect for him is respect to you. He should always tell those he loves how important you are, and this will, in turn, change the level of commitment you have to each other. If he does not stand for you, he will fall away from you.

## Don't date him if you must do anything to make him love you.

Love should come naturally. Most men, if they are in love, will tell you they knew it right away. The last thing you want to do is waste your time on a guy who is waiting for the right girl. If you are the one, he will tell you, and he will show it. He may not express his undying love right away, but he will let you know that he digs you. As stated earlier, there are three kinds of girls: friends with benefits, filler girls, and girlfriends. Men do not love filler girls or friends with benefits, and they only use them while they wait for the right partner. Jerks do not see anything in these girls that inspires them to be permanent fixtures in their lives. However, men love girlfriends and see something in them that inspires them to make them stick around for good. So, make no mistake; if a man loves you, he will tell you.

> ## Don't date him if he seems embarrassed to be with you and your children.

Your children are your appendages. They will be a part of you until you marry them off. Never, ever accept a man who seems too embarrassed of you or your children. Long ago, I began to date a guy while I was pregnant with my ex's baby, although I didn't know at first. When we found out I was pregnant, we decided we still wanted to see each other. I began to show, and he began to shy away in public. When I noticed, I asked him about it, and he told me he was a little uncomfortable because it wasn't his baby. I knew at that moment; we would never make it. It would always be him against my child. I would never do that to my kid.

The guy you should be with should feel proud of you, your achievements, and everything in between. If something about you makes him feel embarrassed to be around you, then he is not the guy.

## Don't date him unless you have become secure with yourself.

People get into a relationship for different reasons. Some women get into a relationship with companionship and security in mind. In most cases, women are guided by their emotions to get into a relationship, and they are not able to determine what they need from the relationship. This can result in someone's heart being broken. The best way to understand what you need from a relationship is to understand yourself. I heard one time that a woman may change at least seven times before the age of 25. I can attest to going through a lot of crazy vicissitudes growing up!

## Don't date him unless you know exactly what you want and what you don't want.

If you were at the best restaurant in your city, you would probably not order something you knew you wouldn't eat. So why do women settle for men with habits they know will make them crazy? The problem with dating someone you know is not good for you is that you may decide that you do not want to give them up. Know and understand yourself! If you have issues that keep getting you into trouble, then work on fixing them. Be sure about what you want out of life and out of a man. Stick to it; don't deviate from it. You oversee your destiny, and you are in charge of whom you fall in love with.

There is no perfect man; you wouldn't always be the perfect girl, but you can weed out a lot of nonsense by sticking firmly to what you want. You know yourself better than anyone else.

The only way to know what you want and what you will not put up with is to put yourself out there. I know of so many women who refuse to date any longer because of the bad experiences they have had with men. The truth is that you will only be able to reach Mr. Right when you go through a whole lot of Mr. Wrongs.

The Mr. Wrongs and Mr. Mistakes of your life will be the ones telling you what you want from relationships. So, if you want to settle into a happy relationship, one which gives you exactly what you need, you must be willing to find him.

DON'T
DATE HIM

10

## Don't Date Him If He is Missing Too Many Teeth.
## (Respect Yourself)

> Don't date him if he is missing too many teeth.

Various things influence a person's personality, like teeth and clothes. One can know whether a man is genuine or not by examining his teeth or way of dressing. Once, a friend talked me into going out with her husband's cousin, even though I was not interested. He was severely overweight and missing a lot of teeth. Is there anything wrong with dating overweight men? Heck no! I love bear hugs, but back to his teeth. He was missing more than a few. That should have been my clue that he might have a personality issue. He kept stating that he was a hustler and he would be one until the day he died. He told me he was in sales and that he owned his own business. I continued to see him whenever I saw my friend at her home. I eventually started to go out with him, and I eventually found out what kind of sales he was in - drugs.

## Don't date him if he doesn't like your friends.

The man you date should like your friends, as they are part of you unless they have a bad influence on you. If your man does not like your friends, then there might be a good reason why he doesn't, and you should ask him why (sounds redundant).

Watch out for this one, friends. I was dating my ex-husband when I met a new friend. I liked this girl, and I wanted us to become good friends. She was charismatic and funny, just like me. For some reason, unbeknownst to me, my ex hated this girl and could never give me a good reason. They screwed. Enough said.

## Don't date him if your friends can give you a valid reason not to.

No one knows you like your buddies. Now and then, a friend may get jealous of your new relationship and may even display a little hatred of your new beau because she is losing a friend. But a good friend knows what you need before you even know sometimes. They can see things you can't. Don't date a man who your family and friends dislike because he might be a loser. Your family and friends can see things that you aren't always able to see. Maybe the guy hit on her, and she doesn't want to tell you. Maybe she knows he is hurting you. Or, maybe she knows you can do better. Your family and friends are honest, and emotions like yours do not cloud their judgment.

## Don't date him if he already has more than three baby mamas.

"Baby Daddy" drama is one thing, but "Baby Mama" drama is oh, so tiresome. The guy with a whole lot of baby mamas was probably not faithful to any of them. This is a sign that he doesn't plan for the future and does not give a damn about who gets hurt in his pursuit to get laid. Unfortunately, the children are the ones who truly suffer.

## Don't Date Him If He is of a Different Religion than You Are.
## (Religion & Morals)

Don't date him if he is of a different religion than you are.

Religion and culture play a chief role in any relationship. Some communities encourage their children to date and marry people from within their religion to keep their culture and religion alive. Also, the communities inspire children to date people from their religion to maintain their families into the future. Religious differences can affect relationships and families because parents are not able to raise their families harmoniously if they have different beliefs and values.

Unfortunately, there are many wars that are caused because of religious differences.

Making sure both you and your partner have the same belief systems are important in raising your family.

One of my favorite things to do is to eat out. I had a roommate named Angel, who was a devout Jehovah's Witness. I had a date with a man who took me to Perry's Steakhouse. The filet was mouthwatering, so I saved a piece for Angel to try. I heated the steak and cut the first piece to feed to her. She said, "Mmm," then looked down at rest and spat it out. I sometimes enjoy my steak medium rare. This was a sin for her as she was not supposed to ingest any other blood. She began to spit it out. I had to apologize for an hour. I know Angel and I did not date, but why waste your time in the battle with someone that has strong beliefs that you do not agree with.

## Don't date him if he does things that go against your morals.

Different cultures have different norms, and members are supposed to adhere to the norms of the society. What might seem bad in one culture might not be wrong in another.

Morals are the principles and values that guide a

person's actions or a group of people. They tend to keep people together and generally result in outward behavior acceptable by concerned parties.

There is a high possibility that conflicting morals would result in distaste in a relationship regardless of how tolerating both parties might be. Differences in their core values would surely bring about challenges.

Members of the society judge others according to the people they associate with and how they behave. Thus, one should date someone who does not do things that are not in line with their morals. Dating someone who, let's just say, breaks the law, would go against my morals. People tend to associate you with who you hang out with. I understand there is a desire to date the "bad boy." Now that I am an adult, my character and how people see me are essential. I have a friend who's a police officer. Her husband was very much into physical fitness, and he was also into the selling of illegal steroids. When he got busted (and they always get busted), she had to either divorce him or quit her career. She left her profession. She will always be associated with the husband, who is a felon. She will always be the source of speculation.

## Don't date him if he won't wait for you when you have chosen celibacy.

People who wait to have sex after marriage have a higher percentage rate of success. That's a fact. I had a friend who recently got married. When she had questions about sex, I was surprised and amazed that she had waited to have sex until marriage. I was thrilled and honored to tell her what she needed to know. I was also so proud of her because it is tough to find people who wait to get married before having sex. I am currently practicing celibacy for my spiritual growth. I also stay celibate because I would never want my daughters to think it is OK for men to be running in and out of our home. Set a good example for your children. If a man can't wait for you, then he is not serious about you. A good man will appreciate that you've been waiting just for him. Your romance together will be more magical when you are mental, physical, and spiritually ready.

## Don't date him if you come second to anyone except God.

Men should ensure their partners are a priority in their lives. They should not let their partners come second to anyone other than God. I like to think that I put God first in the decisions I make much of the time. Next, my children fall in the line of importance. Then, everything else. My ex-husband and I once got into a big argument while I was pregnant and didn't want him to go out with his cousin because it was already late in the night, and I didn't want to be alone. He accused me of not wanting him to be with his family. I was his wife, but he wanted to be with his family. Our marriage didn't last, and he is now a forty-year-old living with his mother. It should never be an issue of whom or what is most important to him if he claims to love you. You should never have to guess what he values most. If it's his friends, let him live with them.

## Don't date him if you want children and he doesn't.

Discussing your desire for kids early on in a relationship might feel uncomfortable and premature, but it can become a big deal down the line.

I hear this story so much. Girl falls for the guy. Guy tells the girl he doesn't want children. Girl does want children but submits to this man anyway. Guy and girl get married. Guy cheats with another woman, gets the other woman pregnant, leaves the original girl with a wasted life and childless.

Or, girl stays with guy and gets pregnant anyway, and the man feels betrayed and trapped and blames the woman and his child for the new restraints placed on his life.

This conversation is one you must have. If he resists the idea, first find out the reason for his hesitation. Many variables go into making a relationship work, and big issues like this should be addressed early and clearly. Putting off these kinds of conversations to avoid being misunderstood will cause trouble later.

If you have had a conversation about kids and it becomes clear that one person wants them and the other doesn't, it is a reason not to even start the relationship.

The reality is that if more people had such conversations and ironed out these issues sooner, divorce rates would probably be lower.

## Don't Date Him If His Farts Are Toxic to Your Health (Everything Else)

> Don't date him if his farts are toxic to your health.

This is just one of those things; where I can't say, "I told you so." There was this one guy that I got serious with. One day, I was cooking a nice meal for him. I saw him standing in the hallway after he had just used the restroom. I thought something was wrong, so I went to see why he was just standing in my hallway.

I walked over to where he was and realized I'd walked into a toxic wasteland. I tried not to breathe, but the more I tried, the more of the fart I inhaled. It was like the fart was in my mouth sticking to my now numb tongue! I have never smelled something so ungodly. I gasped, and I dry heaved. My stomach was so upset I couldn't even eat my dinner. I dated him only for a short while after that. He farted all the time after that, and they always smelled horrible.

Let me put it out there; there is no such as fart-shaming. A guy who enjoys constantly letting 'em rip to your disgust and doesn't take your feelings seriously is a lady boner killer. You will have to accept that he isn't the guy who is committed to your comfort.

If he has a habit that bothers you, don't go on a date. At first, you might think that this habit is no big deal but will make you want to bury him alive when you are married. So, do not continue to date someone who has such defiling habits that Satan himself would not want to visit.

## Don't date him if he is into pornography.

I have a problem with mixing fantasy into reality. If a man needs a porno to get off with you, he doesn't get off to you.

You want a man to see you like the sexual being

God made you be, not the Buffy does Houston scenario every time you get together.

If you decide to date this man, don't expect his addiction to go away once your relationship begins (you already know change doesn't happen this way). Married women who have husbands that struggle with porno understand that normal marital sexual relations can't take the place of porn in his life. Why then do you think you will be different?

This is because pornography addiction transcends sex. It's a symptom of intimacy disorder – a psychological condition that causes an individual to avoid meaningful interactions with humans and to replace it with impersonal sexual imagery.

I know of guys that are incapable of having sex without a porn flick on in the background. Porn can affect relationships as men are not interested in a relationship and sex. You should drop a man who is into pornography if you tell him how the porn affects you and he continues to watch it. You should look for a man who understands you and wants to see only you instead of any other woman. This will help you save your marriage in the future.

## Don't date him if he talks dirty all the time.

I started dating this cowboy. He seemed like a stand-up gentleman and was excited about dating this guy because we had some of the same ideas about relationships and raising children. One day, I got a text from him in the middle of the day while I was at work. He was saying some really perverted things.

I was in shock as I read his text. He never spoke this way in person! I asked him to please not say things like that while I was at work with children. He continued, telling me I was way too reserved. Even though he knew that I worked with kids, he refused to stop texting me nasty messages. After a couple of more days of those texts, I sent him a break-up text and kept my phone off for the remainder of the year at work. I would never want my children or students to read something like that sent to me.

## Don't date him if he wants to take you to his favorite strip club.

My Facebook friend, Adriana, posted this story about a date she had. "When I was 21, and in my partying phase of life, I was asked out on a date by a co-worker who was a nice guy. When the night came for our date, I asked him what the plans were for the evening, and he said a group of us would be going out to eat and then hitting some clubs afterward, but first, we were going to Rick's. Being the utterly naïve person back in the day, I assumed we were going to his friend's house. So, the evening arrived, and my friend came to pick me up, and off we drove, nicely dressed, to go to his friend's house. Well, to my surprise, we started pulling up before a strip club, Rick's in Richmond!

My heart dropped, and I felt like I'd been bamboozled, but in reality, I hadn't; it was just my ignorance! As we were parking, I asked my friend, "Is this really where we're going?" and he nonchalantly answered, "Yeah, I told you that." It was at that very moment that any naïveté I had suddenly left, and guilt replaced it. I told him I couldn't go in thinking of my church and private school upbringing. I argued with him for a couple of minutes until he finally said, "It'll be fun, you'll see." Not wanting to be the party pooper on our date, I relented. I was in shock just entering and seeing the women on stage with boozed-up men all around. I'd never seen anything like it. We proceeded to the VIP area. For a first date, this was definitely the worst thing he could have done.

## Don't date him if you are both messy people.

The last thing I need in life is a man just like me. I can just foresee major chaos if I found someone like me, but with a penis. With that being said, I would definitely love to go out with a man that had the same taste in TV and movies as I do. We would never have to fight about whose night it was to control the flat screen. People always say opposites attract, and this is for a good reason. For instance, I am a messy person. I hate to clean. My life goal is to be able to afford a maid. For me, to date someone just as messy as me would be tragic! I have a great love for tidy guys and believe it is great if a couple can complement each other.

I am a founder of a non-profit organization, and if I were to hire someone with the same skill as me, we probably wouldn't advance as we needed to. My goal is always to hire someone who has the skills that I lack to complement my strengths with his/her own. I would use them to teach me subjects I am weak in to make my corporation stronger. You should date someone who makes you a better, stronger person.

## Don't date him if he repeats everything his mother says.

Men should listen to their partners if they love them. If a man loves you, he will listen to your needs and will want to know how you are feeling. If a man loves you, he will listen to your advice instead of ignoring you and listening to what other people have to say, including his mother. If a man is not interested in your thoughts and goals, he is not someone you can make a life with. I don't care if you date this guy or not, but it just really gets on my nerves when a man repeats everything his mother says when you have just told him the same thing. I once went out with a guy that got a stain on his favorite jersey and was worried that the stain would not come off. I told him to put a little Dawn on it and scrub it with a toothbrush. He refused to believe that it would work. He called his mother; she told him, "Put a little Dawn on it and scrub it." He told me what his mother said and immediately went and tried it, completely forgetting I had told him the same thing hours ago.

Sigmund Freud told us about men looking for their mothers in their adult heterosexual relationships, but if the guy you are dating cannot go 2 hours without making a reference to his mother, then you should reconsider continuing dating this guy.

## Don't date him if he's just gotten out of a relationship.

You should not date men who have just gotten out of a relationship. Most of the men who have just gotten out of a relationship pretend to love their new partners and flatter them with sweet words, but they do not love them. There are various reasons why such men get into a relationship. First, they get into a relationship to forget their past experiences. Second, they get into relationships to prove to their partners that even if their relationship did not work, their current relationship would work. Third, such men get into a relationship because they do not want to be lonely and hence use their new partners to keep themselves busy.

I hate to admit it, but I am the guilty one here. My divorce was just finalized, and I decided to start dating right away. I met a very handsome guy that I would email, chat with, and talk to on the phone. I had called him a couple of times, and he did not return my calls right away. I noticed he was in the chat but not returning my calls. After a bottle of wine, I sent him an ugly email. We hadn't even gone on a date yet! When I realized what I had done, I was so embarrassed. I wanted to bury my head under my couch. I concluded that the effects of my marriage were still a hindrance to my mental state and that I needed more time to heal.

Men who have just gotten out of a relationship fall fast in love and fast out of love. He will be quick to tell you how much he loves you before you start dating. Telling you he loves you quickly is a worrisome sign as he might not know what true love is and be in love with the idea of being in love rather than being in love with the actual person. A healthy, healed man should be able to wait before falling in love with another person.

## Don't date him if you can see yourself killing him.

You should be careful with the kind of men you date. Do not date men who are jealous and do not trust you, as this can affect your relationship and cost you your life or his life. Trust is important in any relationship as it determines the success of the relationship. Couples should trust each other and should not be overcome by jealousy. Some people thrive on the excitement of a passionate relationship. Some people long for that Romeo and Juliet type of love. I once had a friend who was very honest when she said: "One of us will kill each other." This couple's dysfunction was rooted in jealousy, and they would hit each other until they were bleeding. They refused to leave each other, and my friend would always say, "One day he will kill me, but I don't care; I love him." I had to quit being friends with both of them. That was just too much intense for me. You should stay away from a person who can make you angry enough to want to disable them. Why go anywhere near that?

Besides, does orange look good on anyone?

## Don't date him if he has poor hygiene.

A man who does not clean up and groom himself on the regular is difficult to remain attracted to. Besides, if he can't take care of himself, what else can't he take care of?

Taking baths, wearing clean underwear, clean nails, good breath are just a few required social norms that we can all appreciate. Guys may not mind sweat and grime, so when they are "out with the boys" they can be as dirty and stinky as they want, but they need to clean up once they are with you.

It's one thing for a man to skip deodorant for a day. It's an entirely different thing if they give you the impression that they don't have to properly clean up after using the loo.

It's certainly no small issue dating a man with poor hygiene. If his hygiene is off-putting, bring it up. If it can be resolved, then it's a good sign that you are also compatible.

On the other hand, if you put your views across diplomatically as opposed to being judgmental, and he doesn't budge, leave him right there and move on.

Do not date someone who thinks you do not deserve to see his grime-free face.

**DON'T**
DATE HIM

13

## Don't Date Him If He Views Relationships as a Trap

You meet a guy who is everything you have ever wanted. Six feet tall, smells great and has great listening skills. He seems to be good at everything. There is only one problem, though. He views relationships as a trap. Yeah, he considers relationships to be constricting. He even tells you he has watched a ton of his friends get in and get out of relationships with sorry tales.

What does that tell you about him? He has a commitment phobia! And what should you do? You should know that by now.

*Don't date him.*

## Don't date him if he doesn't see a future with you.

The whole point of dating is to figure out if you have a shot with that person. It is an opportunity to get to know someone to decide whether they are somebody you see yourself growing old next to.

And if you do, congratulations! And if he doesn't, run.

Guys can keep you hanging around forever as they decide if you are worthy of being settled down with or not. They can take as much time as they would like, except it is wrong to waste your time. So, if you find yourself getting attracted to someone who has repeatedly told you that commitment is not their forte, then do yourself a favor and check yourself out.

Unless you are looking for a no-strings-attached type of relations, be careful. If that is what you are after, then you may hang out with Mr. I Hate Commitment for as long as you possibly want to.

The thing to remember about commitment is that it is difficult. A successful relationship requires a commitment to be present in abundance. If you are committed to someone, you will freely give them your time, love, and attention. You would not be telling them that they are needy or they are too demanding.

When you talk about the future, why isn't he just as excited as you are? Men may not be as expressive or emotional as women, but they still have dreams.

If he saw a life with you in it, he would be excited to tell you those dreams and his plans because they are all part of the future he wants both of you to build together. If he constantly changes the topic whenever you bring it up, rest assured that he only has plans for himself.

Some may lie, telling you he doesn't want to talk about the future because he is focused on the now and doesn't want to make promises he probably can't keep. This is simply a move to keep you from feeling you need or want more – because this is what he doesn't want to give you.

## Don't date him if he doesn't know what he wants.

The world is a confusing place; the last thing you would want to get yourself involved with is someone who is pretty confused himself. Guys who have not figured themselves out are a turn-off for many women. It is okay to be a 20 something and confused, but if you are with a 30 something-year-old man who leaves one thing and starts another consistently, he is not the guy for you.

Also, if a man is confused about one area of his life, what's to say he won't be confused about you too? One minute they think you are the best thing that has ever happened to them, and the next, they are not sure about the two of you as a couple anymore.

You don't really know how to interpret what he's saying, and you're certainly unsure about where to go from here. Can you wait for him to make up his mind? How long would this take? Is waiting for him even the right thing to do?

There is no single answer to these questions in your heart. If he doesn't know what he wants, he is most likely not ready for a relationship. You can't wait on him forever to make up his mind, so you'll have to take the reins and make the decision for yourself.

Consider your priorities. Do you need a guy like this? If you're definite about what you want, give him an ultimatum. He will quickly realize you're not going to wait endlessly whilst he figures things out, and he will give you the answer you need, one way or the other.

Such men come in and go out of women's lives as it is some sort of a God-given right. Guard your heart.

# Don't date him if he considers you are the reason behind his confusion.

We have a bad habit of not working on the inside of ourselves. We spend months and sometimes even years trying to work on our appearances. When it comes to figuring out who we really are, what makes us happy, what we want from life, what adds meaning to our life…we have nothing because all we did was work on the outside of our body to appeal to men.

We are all guilty of not truly working on the insides ourselves. However, if you come across a man who blames you for his confused ways, know that you are not to be held responsible for the fact that he did not do any of the deep, soul-searching work.

Men and women alike must take responsibility for their lives and actions. If he has a habit of pointing fingers at you for his confusion, he is probably going to keep blaming you when other problems arise in your relationship.

You don't need such negativity in your life.

*Don't date him.*

**DON'T**
DATE HIM

14

# Don't Date Him If He Doesn't Know How to Hold a Conversation

There are men out there who might be considered as average looking; however, when they start talking, you cannot help but be mesmerized.

These are the people who know that beauty is more than skin- deep and that one's personality contributes so much to beauty. Personally, I feel that even if the guy is good looking, if he does not know how to carry a conversation, it kills any amount of attraction. Do not date men who are all about answering questions in monosyllables.

Nobody has time for that.

## Don't date him if he is **INTERESTING** but not **INTERESTED**.

On the other hand, you may also come across someone who has to lead an immensely interesting life and is so excited to share it with you. And he does share it with you. And he keeps on sharing it with you.

But when it comes to the part where you get to say something, he cannot help but yawn directly into your face. The guy is impressive, but is he interested in getting to know you?

Not really. And that should be cue enough for you to be interested in one thing only: walking out that door.

Is he doesn't give you his undivided attention when you speak, and he is uninterested in the things that excite you, but he readily goes the distance in telling you how cool he is, the big things he has done with his life, blah blah blah, you have a narcissist right there.

## Don't date him if he is narcissistic:

There is one good reason for not dating a narcissistic: he will love himself more than he will ever love you.

Everything about the relationship will be focused

on him. He will always be the start of the show. A nar-cissistic man can only be happy with someone who is submissive, somebody who would not mind tossing their own needs to the side and completely submitting themselves to his needs.

Every occasionally, we may all need admiration. We all like being told good things about ourselves, but being told stories about our greatness constantly is never fun. Mature men have a healthy sense of self. They do not want to be constantly reminded of how great they are. Who wants to stay seated on a pedestal anyway?

## Don't date him if he doesn't get your sense of humor.

Having a good sense of humor helps when life gets rough. In such situations, taking it easy and laughing at your own mistakes can help lighten the burden. And if you can find someone who gets your sense of humor, then you have found someone to laugh through life with.

It doesn't get any better than this!

Jessica, a friend of mine, was in a relationship with a guy who could not only not understand her jokes but would also put her down for having such a "lame" sense of humor. He will tell her that she needs to "grow up" and be more mature.

So, taking his very "grown up" advice, Jessica did what every "mature" woman should do: She left him.

## Don't date him if he is sarcastic all the time.

Being sarcastic occasionally might make you stand out from others. You may also enjoy a little sarcasm now and then. If the person you are with is sarcastic all the time, it can be a little difficult to have a decent conversation with him. This is because sarcastic people forget to draw a line because they are used to making sarcastic comments when expressing their feelings.

Every time you want his opinion on something, you get a sarcastic answer. Additionally, some men also end up saying hurtful things and then try to soften the blow by saying they were only "kidding." This attitude can cause great harm to you and your relationship and take it south in an instant.

This brings me to my second point: just like you should avoid people who are sarcastic all the time, individuals who joke all the time are equally people you should be a little skeptical about dating. The ability to laugh and make others laugh is truly nothing more than a gift, a talent of sorts, but there are moments where you need to be a little more serious.

All of this reinforces the importance of dating someone who shares your sense of humor. No matter how dark or twisted or happy and full of rainbows your humor is, if you have a partner who gets it, you are set.

## Don't date him if he asks you to give up on things he doesn't like.

Part of being with someone is to accept them for who they are. If the guy you have started dating has a problem with you reading too much, it is time to start walking.

The way I see it, if you want to end up in a healthy, successful relationship with someone, you must be supportive of them, their dreams, and their interest even if those things are not your cup of tea. You love that person, and their interests are what make them so unique. So, the next time you go on a date with a guy who has a problem with you wearing too much makeup, put on some more lipstick and walk away from him.

## Don't date him if he has no ambitions.

A man with no motivations is an annoying man. He has no aims and no goals that he sees himself achieving. If nothing else, you might have great chemistry, and he could be ambitious about being with you.

What would be sweeter than that?

All jokes aside, men with no ambitions seem to take life a little too easy. And real life is difficult; sometimes, a fight in life is necessary.

You deserve someone with the same drive as you or a stronger motivation than you. Your desire for a partner who challenges you to do great things is valid; you don't need someone who will pull you down to his level of lethargy.

A relationship is a partnership; it could quickly become a situationship if you choose to date a guy with no ambitions.

**DON'T**
DATE HIM

**15**

# Don't Date Him If He Rushes Things with You

I touched on this topic earlier in the book; however, I soon realized that I had more to say on this subject and hence, decided to have an entire chapter just for this.

If a guy rushes things with you, it only means one thing: he is hiding something. There are certain people you will know better in 7 days than you will know someone else in seven years. While this is true, it is important to take it slow when it comes to the matters of the heart. The only way to get to know someone is to spend time with them, and the more time you spend with someone, the better you get to know if the two of you can have a shot at making it together in the future.

So, if you come across a guy who cannot wait to rush to you down the aisle, tell him you appreciate his enthusiasm, but you need him to slow it down, and you need more time to decide if the two of you are truly meant for each other or not. In order not to regret your decisions later, it is best you take time before making them.

I have also heard of many cases where guys are so intense and come on so strong at the beginning of the relationship…only to dump the girl later. What went wrong here? It was not love, it was infatuation or maybe just lust, and it was misinterpreted. The guy finally realizes this and goes cold. Whereas many times, the girls involved in such situations are already so far in, it is difficult not feeling heartbroken when the phone calls suddenly stop. This again reinforces the point I was trying to make that even if the guy, very early on, starts referring to you as his "girlfriend" because "the chemistry is so off the charts," you take your time in deciding where you stand with him.

Do it for your sake.

## Don't date him if he guilt trips you into saying those three words.

Despite the juvenile and exasperating nature of guilt trips, they are all too common in relationships nowadays. In fact, most romantic relationships are susceptible to them.

There are guys you will meet who will be so smitten with you that they would not be able to help themselves, and they spout out those three words way too fast.

Because they crave acceptance from you, they may decide to take the manipulative route. So, essentially, they try to make you feel guilty for how nice and supportive they have always been of you and of all that you do, and yet here you are, not loving them back.

Love cannot be forced, but I have seen these guys work their magic on women in making them feel so terrible that they start feeling that maybe they are as shallow as the guys point out.

And because you want to avoid upsetting the balance of the relationship, you give in to the feeling of guilt and the need to please him, and you end up saying "I love you too" in return which never seems to work out in the long run because you do not *really* love them. Naturally, when tough times pop up, you will always want to have a way out of that relationship.

## Don't date him if he uses your feelings as a ticket to get his way with things.

Mr. Wrong: "If you loved me, you would do this for me."

Sensible, Intelligent Woman: "If you loved me, you would not be asking me to do things that I am not comfortable doing."

It is plain ridiculous how many times I have heard men saying to their women that if they loved them, they would let them do this or that. Relationships have a lot to do with patience and compromise, and there will be times where you must forgive or ignore your partner's shortcomings, but if this becomes a regular habit where he uses your love as a "get-out-of-mess" card, you need to give him a "get-out-of-my-life" card.

## Don't date if he is hot one second and cold the next.

Jane had been friends with Greg for two years before her last boyfriend cheated on her, so she became drawn to Greg. They started going out, and he treated her so well. After six months, she told him she was getting cold feet about jumping into another relationship too soon. She wanted to date other people, but she continued seeing Greg.

Realizing he had the qualities she wanted in a man, she made a commitment to him.

At first, he was the most caring and sweetest man. However, as the relationship progressed, Greg began to act like he was superior to her. He called her names and became very short tempered.

This went on for a while as she tried to be the patient girlfriend. Whenever he lost his temper, she would be very loving and pamper him. When he acted obnoxiously and abused her, she would cry, and he would tell her she was too old for that. They discussed this many times, and she would tell him that he needed to stop being cruel to her. He would apologize and promise never to do it again.

One minute, they would be the happiest couple in the world, the next minute, he would remind her that she made him wait while she dated other people, and the name calling would continue.

If you are an optimist, you might find unpredictability to be helpful. It keeps things interesting and keeps you on your toes because you never know what is coming next, but imagine dating someone who is into you one second and the next acts as if you do not exist.

No one should go through all of these or be made to endure such headache. You don't have to tiptoe around your partner for fear of starting another fight. His actions are simply inexcusable.

If you have never complained about getting headaches, you are about to now. If he can't admit that he has a problem and is committed to changing, the best thing you can do is to leave the situation.

If you choose to date him, you are encouraging and reinforcing unhealthy behaviours as well as hurting your own self-esteem.

Remember, you can't change a man; your behaviors are the only ones you have control over.

## Don't date him if he is emotionally selfish.

One reason why some guys are quick to hurry things along with the women they are dating is that they focus just on their emotions while completely disregarding the women. They meet a woman who they hit it off well with, and only a short while later, they decide that she is the one because they feel that way, rather than consulting his partner.

Is the woman on board with their plan for this sudden commitment to? No, and for emotionally selfish men, it is not necessary that she should be, either. If the emotionally selfish man is getting something, he is okay. Dating such a man is never a good idea because every time you feel something about a particular issue and try to bring it up with him, he would blatantly ignore it because it does not concern his emotions.

**DON'T**
DATE HIM

16

# Don't Date Him If He Acts His Shoe Size and Not His Actual Age

In this chapter, we will be talking about the infamous Man- Child. Someone who is an adult but does not want to act like one. And we get it. It's fun being a kid. No responsibilities. Less drama. No diets. But are these guys entertaining to date?

Absolutely not! As it is, one must do a lot to keep one's self in check, and now you are expected to do someone else's work, even when they are perfectly able to manage things on their own? I briefly dated a guy who fits perfectly into this criterion. I quickly learned that he was hardly serious about any plans he would make, had no real ambition within 10 miles around him, and was pretty put off by ambitious women too. Such a man is still pretty much in the "patriarchal" mindset, so naturally, when they see a woman who is accomplishing more than he is, he feels insecure. If only he would start bothering less about the ambitions of others and be more bothered about his lack of it.

## Don't date him if someone else shops for him.

Continuing with dating men who refuse to take responsibility for their lives, do not date a man who does not shop for himself and is proud of it.

Plenty of heterosexual men applaud themselves for not getting interested in fashion but what they should not be applauding for is having someone else pick all their clothes for them, predominantly, if this other person updating their wardrobe is their mother.

Run away.

Mothers are awesome, and they always continue being awesome, but dating a guy who has his mother pick out everything from him, from his shirts to his boxers, is borderline creepy.

## Don't date him if he does not own up to his mistakes.

Making mistakes is the quickest, most efficient way of learning, but in the dating pool, you will come across men who will not learn from their mistakes because they refuse to accept that they even made a mistake in the first place.

We are not immune to errors, and misunderstandings may happen, but if in an argument and you are the only one constantly apologizing, you need to stop. You do not need to date someone who does not have the courage to accept that he made an error and make amends for it.

I have read in many advice columns where relationship experts tell committed couples to toss their ego on the side and accept their mistakes to save their relationship even if it was not their fault. While the bit about tossing your ego on the side is not that bad of advice, I commonly believe that you do not have to completely part ways with your sense of self-respect. Hold on to it and when you come across a man who waits for you to apologize even if it is not your fault, then tell him that the only thing you are only going to apologize for is wasting all that time on him.

## Don't date him if he constantly brings up that one selfless act he did

Imagine dating a guy who, every time something bad happens, brings up that one kind thing he did for you and then tries to dig his way out. He could have done that one nice thing ages ago, but he does not wait two seconds to bring it right up every time you tell or accuse him of slacking off on matters concerning you.

Dating someone like that would mean you are forever indebted to that favor he did. Even worse is that sometimes you may not even know that he is doing something nice, not out of courtesy for you but because he wanted to keep something in his back pocket so he could use it against you. You tell him how he never helps around with things, and he would remind you of that one time he set up the printer for you.

## Don't date him if he views your confidence as self-obsession

Your confidence can be misinterpreted for many things. Dating a guy who, instead of admiring your spirit, constantly reprimands you for being too full of yourself needs to get away from you. In a world where we are constantly surrounded by people who are ever willing and available to point out your flaws and make you feel insecure, the last thing you would want is to get romantically involved with someone like that as well.

## Don't date him if he treats love like a game.

We all love games, but if the game requires your emotions, then you should look for the nearest exit. If the guy you are dating plays with your feelings, it only means that he is not serious about you.

Perhaps you met someone who swept you off your feet with something beyond his looks and charisma. You spend time discussing topics you ordinarily don't share talk about so quickly.

You start believing in love and having some hope in humanity. You begin to feel you are gravitating towards something serious with this guy.

Suddenly, it seems this man you connected deeply with starts sending mixed signals. One minute, he is all over you, and the next, he doesn't take your calls. He tells you he is nervous about putting a label on your relationship and gives myriads of reasons he can't have you around.

He is most likely not invested in you. If this is the

case, you need to move far away from him while you can. If he is not serious about you, there is no need to continue seeing him.

If, at any moment in time, a guy gives you the impression that he is manipulating you or taking you for a ride – even if he is still interested in you, don't date him.

## Don't date him if he always wants to stay in.

Dating someone who always wants to stay in and never really does anything fun can only work out if you are also an introvert. Still, even if you are introverted and being in the great outdoors is not your thing, being in a relationship with a man who just wants to stay in bed and not take you out may mean that he is just into you for sex.

## Don't date him if he has no real opinions of his own.

It's quite refreshing to date a guy who agrees with your viewpoints. The alarm bells should go off if you realize he is extremely passive, he won't take a stance, and he leaves you to make all the plans and decisions.

I dated a man who was so easily influenced by what others had to say about a topic that he never actually stated his own opinions. All his views and his opinions were borrowed. Dating someone like that is a drag because you never really get to know how he thinks about something. Also, such people are never able to hold their ground. They are quick to believe everything someone else does without even questioning it or reasoning it out.

For a moment, imagine settling down with this guy; after working on an assignment with your kids, you tell them to share it with their dad, then they say, "No, we won't do that. Dad never says anything about anything. He never has an opinion about anything."

You'll agree with me that this will be a problem in the future – one you can nip in the bud right now.

You need to date a man, not a sheep.

**DON'T**
DATE HIM

**17**

## Don't Date Him If He is a Bad Boy

The reason is simple. Don't date bad boys because, well, they are *bad*.

From the law to your heart, there is nothing these guys will not break, and you do not need any of that. As someone who has been there and done that, let me be the first one to assure you that this whole "dating a bad boy" is blown way out of proportion. There is nothing nice about being with a guy who does not respect you or your feelings or the law.

A friend once dated a guy we called a "bad boy." She told us much about their relationship. It was exciting for a few months but got horrible after that. The guy was more interested in everything but her. She soon found out he wasn't only cheating on her; he peddled drugs. The relationship ended after years of suffering for her.

Women who are attracted to bad boys hope for the best by believing they will find a bad boy who is only good for them. After all, what could be better than a guy who blows off everyone except you? But the chances of you coming across someone like that are pretty slim. Most bad boys are just what they are: BAD.

## Don't date him if he makes you chase him.

It's fine to play it cool when you finally meet a guy who genuinely loves you. While you shouldn't downplay or conceal your feelings, you shouldn't be chasing him and doing all the work.

Real men don't need to be play games or be chased. A man who knows your worth won't be able to keep himself from you long enough for you to begin to see the need to chase him. Real happiness comes from being happy with yourself and allowing the right people in and around your life, not because you went after them.

If you come across a guy who plays hard to get, leave him alone. You have got nothing to prove by winning the attention or concern of such a person. You do not need that kind of validation from dating a man who does not believe in being with you; it is a perk on its own.

If attention is not given free and on its own, then it is not worth having it. If he's the one for you, you'll not have to chase him.

## Don't date him if he thinks the mystery is a good thing.

Part of the whole bad boy charm is their mysterious aura they seem to have around them all the time. What do we do with mysteries? We try to solve them.

And while you are solving them, you come across all these things, facts, stories, and secrets surrounding them, which may not always be positive. So, if you come across a guy who does not "give too much" away about his "self" because he feels that being mysterious is cool, you should reconsider dating him.

If he is acting mysterious, it could mean that he is hiding something which he does not want you to know. So really, ask yourself if you are willing to put your heart on the line just to solve the mystery of the bad boy.

## Don't date him if you are the only one holding on to him.

Dating, like marriage and trust, is a two-way road. It has to be this way. If you are the only one planning dates, showing interest, and making all the effort, you are clearly with the wrong person.

Also, you should hold him to the same expectations as you hold yourself. If he is giving less than one hundred percent to the relationship in terms of his effort, take the cue and dump him.

Bad boys are called bad for a reason.

## Don't date him if he is only into booty-calls.

How to spot a booty caller? The easiest way to spot someone who only dates women for just one reason and one reason alone is to look for just one sentence "I am not like *those* guys."

First off, who are "those guys"? And what is wrong with those guys that he so specifically does not want to be associated with them? Whatever answers to those questions you may come up with, let me tell you something I learned from my own experience.

I once dated a guy who was very adamant about the fact that he is not the type of guy who is only into hooking up with women. However, oddly enough, our date conversations seemed to always revolve around our looks.

He hardly ever complimented me on anything else. And it had not been that long since we had begun dating that he started texting me at the oddest hours of the night, asking if I could come over to his place, or he could come over to mine.

So, when someone tells me that they are not one of those guys, a little voice inside my head starts saying, "you most definitely may be one of those guys."

Look for a man who has a clear agenda and does not lie about it. If he is dating someone just to get in their pants, then he should be open about it because there are plenty of women out there who prefer a no-strings-attached relationship.

The number one rule to dating anybody is to remember not to lie about who you are and what you want. Honesty is the best policy!

DON'T
DATE HIM

18

# Don't Date Him If He is All Talk and No Work

Just like you should avoid dating the Man Child and the Booty Caller, you should also actively avoid the Big Talker.

A big talker is somebody who makes plans but never follows through. He tells you that he will do this, and that other thing you once talked about, but here is the catch: he never does it.

Such a person has these grand ideas for the two of you as a couple which is fantastic to hear, but guess what would be even more fantastic? Him doing those things! There is a very valid reason why I ask women to avoid getting into a relationship with the guy who just has words to offer you but no real action. The reason is that men are practical human beings, naturally.

They do things. Doing things that give them a sense of achievement, so if you come across someone who has all the right words but has major difficulties following through, he is not serious about you. At most, he is just leading you on.

He is not doing something because he does not *want* to do it.

## Don't date him if he has his head in the clouds.

The guy you should be dating should be somebody who has realistic views about the world. If you are with someone who dreams of doing great things but has no real plans and strategies on how to get from point A to point B, they are only going to disappoint.

The thing about Big Talkers is that they are so good with words! They manage to convince you from time and time again that they will do that thing they have been promising you. Somehow you always manage to stay, thinking at the back of your mind that maybe this time he will come around.

No, he will not come around, but you can get over him.

## Don't date him if he is living in the past.

Guys who only talk about how great their past was and how their present can never compete with it seem to forget one crucial detail: You exist in the present.

Something from their glorious past is brought up in almost every conversation you have with them. It is frustrating if nothing else. If they feel that their past was so much better than their present, then why do they not work on improving the here and now?

## Don't date him if he is the out of sight, out of mind type.

You may have a super busy routine, and you cannot squeeze in as many dates as you might want to. The guy you are dating does not understand your work commitments and instead only acts interested when you are around. But when you are not around, he acts as if you do not even exist. He is always super charming and amazing when you are sitting next to him, but he is charming and amazing with someone else every time you are not with him. The right man will always be interested in you, whether or not you are around.

## Don't date him if he twists your words.

I have repeatedly mentioned how communication is such an important part of any relationship throughout this book. No matter how amazing the person you are dating is, if there are problems in how you communicate as a couple, the relationship will not last long.

Problems in communication are not just related to not being able to find the right words for what you want to say, or using the wrong kind of tone; sometimes you might say the right thing, using the right words and tone at the perfect time and still find yourself in a mess.

What went wrong there? The guy you were communicating with got what you were saying loud and clear, but still, there is miscommunication. Fortunately, the error is not on your part, but unfortunately, you will still have to pay the price, that is, if you want to.

Guys who twist your word repeatedly just want to make you look bad and do not deserve a second of your time. Such men like stirring up unnecessary trouble. They will twist your words around so much that your message will seem to be conveying an entirely different message than what was originally intended to say.

## Don't date him if there is no consistency between his words and actions.

Do not date men whose words say one thing while their actions tell a completely different story. Such people are so confusing, and you never know where you stand with them. They tell you that they are interested in getting to know you better, except they keep on canceling dates at the last minute.

And if you are ever feeling confused and question what to believe, his words or actions, then remember that men are rational beings and practicality has everything to do with taking action. So, if he keeps flaking on you despite telling you that he is interested, he is not.

## Don't date him if he has selective attention.

Guys with selective attention can also be extremely difficult to be with because they only pay attention to things that concern them or those that interest them.

If you bring up concerns that you're pretty sure are

not unreasonable, and he does and says nothing about them, he is not worth dating.

If you are looking for a long term happy relationship, you need to find yourself someone who pays attention to everything you say because everything you say is important. It is impossible always to do things that the guy likes, and you must share interests.

## Don't date him if he is always misunderstanding you.

If the guy you are currently with seems more committed to misunderstanding you than he is into you generally, you need to find yourself someone who will take the time to understand you better. We all have our priorities, and even if you have found a person who looks exactly like your dream guy but never understands who you are and who you will be soon is not worth your time. If you are young, sometimes you have not yet become who you will be. You need to take the time to understand yourself, and if this guy truly wants to date you, he will take the time to help you figure it out.

## Don't date him if he gets defensive all the time.

This is a continuity of the point mentioned above; guys who misunderstand you are also more likely to get defensive about things even if those things were nothing to get worked up about. Again, such men are difficult to converse with. You have to walk on eggshells around them constantly. It is advised that you should think before you speak, but if you have to weigh in every word, every syllable before you can say something to the man you are with, you need to reevaluate your situation.

I cannot possibly explain how beautiful it is to find someone you could just be yourself with.

## Don't Date Him If He is Separated

Dating a divorcee is different than dating a man who is separated. If you happen to catch feelings for a separated man, you might want to retrace your steps, and here is why. He is still married. And that, in turn, could mean a lot of things. He may not be living with his wife under the same roof, his wife may be seeing other men too, but that does not change the fact that he is still married. If you see him as somebody you could be involved with, then at least wait for the divorce to be finalized.

I urge all my readers to wait until things have finalized because dating a man who is separated can mean that he is keeping you as a secret. He would not want to be seen with you in public, which could be very hurtful.

I say this with experience. I dated a man who was separated, but he hadn't yet followed up with the divorce settlement. He was a very nice man, easy to talk to and very interesting. The only problem was that every time we would hang out, he would suggest that we do it at our place or in some area on my side of the neighborhood.

He did not want someone from his circle to spot him with me. He did eventually confess that to me, and once he did, I never saw him again. You do not need to keep your relationship in the dark.

Another major downside of dating a separated but not divorced yet man is that you will be viewed less as a potential romantic interest and more as his divorce counselor. He will always be telling you details about his marriage and how his almost-but- not-quite-ex-wife always brought his wrong side out. Date someone who is available. Completely available.

## Don't date him if he is not a good father.

The guy you are dating has kids from his ex. While his kids are adorable, he never sees them, hardly talks about them, never shows up on their birthdays, and is basically invisible in their lives.

The guy does not want to take responsibility for his children. Even if he is no longer with the mother of those kids, those kids are still his children and still very much his responsibility. His behavior with his current children could tell you a lot more about what kind of a person he is and what his values are.

There is another scenario for this. One of the worst things I have ever done was to date someone who did not like my children.

He was counting the days for them to move out and was constantly looking for opportunities to upset them. Two of my kids were not even 18 yet, and he was making decisions about when they would move out. Nothing is more important than your children. No man is worth damaging your precious jewels. Yes, children can be difficult, but they are a part of you. If he can't handle them, it may not be the right timing for your relationship.

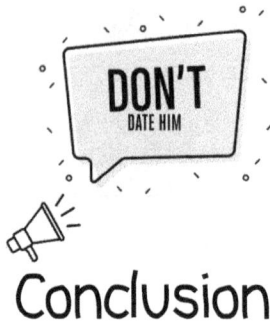

# Conclusion

Dating is difficult, and with so many different types of men out there, you may never know what and whom you will come across.

The various scenarios presented in this book seem like I am asking you to cancel out every guy present on Earth, but in truth, if you are with someone who does any of these things, chances are that he is not the one for you. You have settled for somebody less than you deserve. There are good men out there, men who, despite having had a very troubled childhood, very bad relationships with women of their own, do not pass the torch forward. They stop that vicious circle by being a gentleman to the women in their lives. They make an effort; they make time, they support you, and they always respect your wishes. Since we are human beings and neither of us, women or men can be totally without fault; there will be some flaws in the man you are dating. Mr. Right will not be flawless, but instead, every time he messes up, he will genuinely apologize and see to it that it does not happen again.

What I want my readers to keep in mind is to not strive for perfection but for excellence. If you get put down for being a woman who has way too high standards, tell them that it is simply because you deserve to be with someone who knows what he has when he has you. It is hard not to be picky with the men you date, considering they might end up being a very real part of your life.

I encourage all the women looking for love to know precisely what they want from their ideal man and then fearlessly go in pursuit of it.

If you have had bad experiences with men, please, do not give up on love. There are wonderful people out there.

You just have not met them yet.